BOUND FOR
THE
EAST INDIES

BOUND FOR THE
EAST INDIES

Halsewell
A Shipwreck that Gripped the Nation

ANDREW NORMAN

Fonthill Media Limited
www.fonthillmedia.com
office@fonthillmedia.com

First published in the United Kingdom
and the United States of America 2020

British Library Cataloguing in Publication Data:
A catalogue record for this book is available from the British Library

Copyright © Andrew Norman 2020

ISBN 978-1-78155-753-2

The right of Andrew Norman to be identified as the author of this work has
been asserted by him in accordance with the Copyright, Designs and Patents
Act 1988.

Typeset in 10.5pt on 13pt Sabon
Printed and bound in England

About the Author

Andrew Norman was born in Newbury, Berkshire, UK in 1943. Having been educated at Thornhill High School, Gwelo, Southern Rhodesia (now Zimbabwe) and St Edmund Hall, Oxford, he qualified in medicine at the Radcliffe Infirmary. He has two children Bridget and Thomas, by his first wife.

From 1972-83, Andrew worked as a general practitioner in Poole, Dorset, before a spinal injury cut short his medical career. He is now an established writer whose published works include biographies of Thomas Hardy, T. E. Lawrence, Jane Austen, Agatha Christie, Enid Blyton, Sir Arthur Conan Doyle, Sir Arthur Pearson, Adolf Hitler, and Robert Mugabe. Andrew was remarried to Rachel in 2005.

By the same author

By Swords Divided: Corfe Castle in the Civil War. Halsgrove, 2003.
Dunshay: Reflections on a Dorset Manor House. Halsgrove, 2004.
Sir Francis Drake: Behind the Pirate's Mask. Halsgrove, 2004.
Thomas Hardy: Christmas Carollings. Halsgrove, 2005.
Enid Blyton and her Enchantment with Dorset. Halsgrove, 2005.
Agatha Christie: The Finished Portrait. Tempus, 2007.
Tyneham: A Tribute. Halsgrove, 2007.
Mugabe: Teacher, Revolutionary, Tyrant. The History Press, 2008.
T. E. Lawrence: The Enigma Explained. The History Press, 2008.
The Story of George Loveless and the Tolpuddle Martyrs. Halsgrove, 2008.
Father of the Blind: A Portrait of Sir Arthur Pearson. The History Press, 2009.
Agatha Christie: The Finished Portrait. Tempus, 2006.

Agatha Christie: The Pitkin Guide. Pitkin Publishing, 2009.
Jane Austen: An Unrequited Love. The History Press, 2009.
Arthur Conan Doyle: The Man behind Sherlock Holmes. The History Press, 2009.
HMS Hood: Pride of the Royal Navy. The History Press, 2009.
Purbeck Personalities. Halsgrove, 2009.
Bournemouth's Founders and Famous Visitors. The History Press, 2010.
Jane Austen: An Unrequited Love. The History Press, 2009.
Thomas Hardy: Behind the Mask. The History Press, 2011.
Hitler: Dictator or Puppet. Pen & Sword Books, 2011.
A Brummie Boy goes to War. Halsgrove, 2011.
Winston Churchill: Portrait of an Unquiet Mind. Pen & Sword Books, 2012.
Charles Darwin: Destroyer of Myths. Pen & Sword Books, 2013.
Beatrix Potter: Her Inner World. Pen & Sword Books, 2013.
T. E. Lawrence: Tormented Hero. Fonthill, 2014.
Agatha Christie: The Disappearing Novelist. Fonthill, 2014.
Lawrence of Arabia's Clouds Hill. Halsgrove, 2014.
Kindly Light: The Story of Blind Veterans UK. Fonthill, 2015.
Jane Austen: Love is Like a Rose. Fonthill, 2015.
Thomas Hardy at Max Gate: The Latter Years. Halsgrove, 2016.

Author's website www.andrew-norman.com

Preface

It was late December 1785, the twenty-fifth year of the reign of King George III, King of Great Britain and King of Ireland,[1] whose empire covered one quarter of the Earth's surface. For the past six weeks the Honourable Company Ship (HCS) *Halsewell*, employed in the service of the Honourable East India Company, had been berthed at Gravesend in Kent (a town situated on the River Thames) as she prepared to embark on her third voyage to the East Indies (the whole of South-East Asia to the east of, and including India).

The timing of her journey was dictated by the times of the monsoon—a seasonal prevailing wind which, in the region of South and South-East Asia, blows from the south-west between May and September (and in a reverse direction between October and April).[2] The voyage was expected to be of at least one year's duration.

Halsewell was just one of many hundreds of vessels which had been in the service of the HEIC since its foundation in the year 1600. In the normal course of events, she would have been expected to serve out her working life before passing unnoticed into the history books. However, this was not to be.

When she set sail, on 1 January 1786, no one could have guessed that her dramatic demise would touch the very heart of the nation: an event of such pathos as to inspire the greatest writer of the age, Charles Dickens, to put pen to paper; the greatest painter of the age, J. M. W. Turner to apply brush to canvas, and the King and Queen to pay homage at the very place where the catastrophe occurred.

For variety, interest, curiosity, and exoticism, artefacts recovered from the wreck (some of which continue to baffle some of the leading forensic marine archaeologists in the land) rival those recovered from Spanish Armada galleons wrecked off the west coast of Ireland two centuries before. Such artefacts, as they continue to be discovered, shed further light both on *Halsewell* herself, and on the extraordinary lives of those who sailed in her.

Acknowledgments

I am grateful to the following persons and organizations.

Rodney Alcock; Penny Allen; Sonia Bacca; John Batchelor; Kaimes Beasley; Mark Beswick; Dorothy Bower; John W. Brown; Ian Carruthers; Colin Chalmers; John Chambers; John Chignoli; Jennett Chisholm; Rachel Church; Jason Cochrane; Sarah Cook; Andrea Cordani; Ed Cumming; Richard Daglish (4 × great-grandson of Captain Richard Peirce); Pip Dodd; Gabriel Dragffy; George Duckett; Bob Errington; Mike Etherington; Jean Fessey; Nicholas Hall; Wally Hammond; Emma Harper; Joanne Hawkins; David Haysom; Kate Hay; Treleven Haysom; George Huish; Mick Humphries; Bill Ingles; Russ Johnson; Sam Johnston; Margaret Jones; Susan Juggins; Monique Kent; Mick Kightley; John King; Dorian Leveque; Reino Liefkes; Michèle Losse; Margaret Makepeace; Ann Manders; Craig Marshall, Rector, Church of St Edward King & Martyr, Goathurst (and Churchwardens); Leah McGowan; Leela Meinertas; Catherine Memain; Matthew Millard; Sally Morgan; Charlie Newman; Ann and John Oldfield; Robin Pingree; Linda Poulsen; Cecilia Powell; Robert Pugh; Martin Robson Riley; David Robinson; Cindy Rodaway; Mark Rodaway OBE; Amanda Rutherford; Justin Saddington; R. J. Saville MBE; Colin Shepherd; Les Smith; Jean Sutton; Lisa Traynor; Gina Turner; Jim Tyson; Dr Ian West; Mark J. West; Reverend Jonathan Wilkes; Eric Youle. (*This is the correct spelling, as will later be explained.)

Apollo: The International Art Magazine, London; British Library (Asia, Pacific and Africa Collections); British Postal Museum and Archive; Cambridge University Library; Chatham Historic Dockyard Trust; Christchurch History

Centre; East India Company Records, British Library; Essex Record Office, Chelmsford, Essex; Dorset History Centre; Hampshire Record Office; HM Coastguard, Dover; HM Coastguard, Portland, Dorset; House of Commons Information Office; House of Lords Information Office; Kingston Archives and Local History Centre, Kingston-upon-Thames, Surrey; Meteorological Office, Exeter; Met. Office National Meteorological Archive, Sowton, Exeter; National Army Museum, London; National Library of Wales; National Maritime Museum, Greenwich and Caird Library; Northampton British Sub-Aqua Club; Poole Central Library; Royal Armouries Museum, Fort Nelson, Fareham; Royal Armouries, Leeds; Royal Artillery Museum, Woolwich; SASC Weapons Collection, Warminster, Wiltshire; Seadart Divers Association; Somerset & Dorset Family History Society; Somerset Archives and Local Studies; Streatham Society Local History Group; Thomas Del Mar Ltd; Tiffin School; United Kingdom Hydrographic Office; The Turner Society; Victoria & Albert Museum.

I congratulate all those who have retrieved artefacts from *Halsewell*, and commend them for having preserved these artefacts and shared their information with others. I thank Valerie Read (widow of David John Allen), for making her late husband's *Halsewell* archive available to me. Photographs taken by Ed Cumming were supplied by Ian Carruthers or by the *Halsewell* Project Group.

I am especially grateful to my beloved wife, Rachel, for all her help and encouragement.

Finally, whereas every effort has been made to trace and obtain permission of those who own the copyright to the artefacts herein illustrated, this has not always been possible to achieve.

CONTENTS

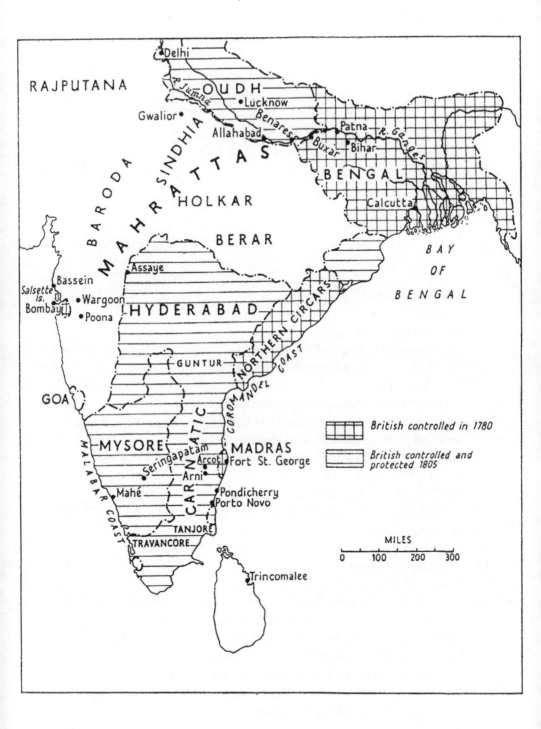

India, from J. Steven Watson, *The Reign of George III.*

Appendices

The Honourable East India Company

The Honourable East India Company (HEIC, or simply 'the Company') came into being, following a meeting held in London in September 1599, presided over by the Lord Mayor when

> ... it was decided to form an association to carry on direct trade with India. Thirty thousand pounds were subscribed, and a petition was exhibited to the Privy Council showing that the merchants of London—induced by the success of the Dutch merchants who had 'made several voyages to some parts of the East Indies and have had returns from thence with their ships richly laden with pepper, spices and other merchandises'—were resolved to make England a staple [place of importance for the importation] of Eastern produce ...[1]

In their petition, the merchants spoke in awe and admiration of

> the most mightie and the [wealthy] Empire of China; the rich and mightie Kingdome of Pegu [a city and river port of southern Burma, on the Pegu river]; the rich and [golden] island of Sumatra; the rich and innumerable islands of the Malucos [Moluccas] and the Spicerie [so-called 'Spice Islands' of Indonesia, Sri Lanka and the coasts of India]; the manifold and populous [silver] islands of the Japones [i.e. Japan].

These places, which were 'abounding in [wealth] and riches', were at present, 'wholly out of the dominion of the Portugalls and Spaniards'.[2]

The outcome was, that on 31 December 1600, Her Majesty Queen Elizabeth I gave her assent to the granting of a charter, which effectively granted the Honourable East India Company a monopoly of trade between London and the East Indies.

> The principal object of those English merchants who in 1600 fitted out a fleet of ships to trade to the East Indies was to obtain for themselves directly all those advantages and profits which up to now had been enjoyed by the Portuguese and Spanish merchants ...[2]

Other rivals to the Company were the French and the Dutch. The Dutch East India Company, for example, which was founded two years later in 1602, established 'factories' (i.e. trading stations) on the Indian subcontinent. 'The Hollanders' had 'got into their possession divers [of varying type] of the chief places of traffic' in the East Indies, namely, the Moluccas Islands of Indonesia—the legendary 'Spice Islands'—and sought 'wholly to debar the English from the trade'.[3] The English view, however, was that 'trade and commerce ought ever to stand free.'

Rivalry between the two companies lead to the First Anglo-Dutch War (1652-54), and although the Dutch were defeated, they nonetheless 'continued to retain their ascendancy in the eastern trade.'[4]

As for the HEIC, an idea of its subsequent scale of operations is gleaned from an account of the sixth voyage of the Company, undertaken in 1609-10, which was

> equipped ... on a scale which they had not yet attempted. £82,000 was subscribed, and they built at Deptford a splendid new vessel, the *Trades Increase*, of 1,100 tons. The king himself [James I] launched it.

HCS *Trades Increase*, commanded by Sir Henry Middleton, dwarfed her two companions *Peppercorn* (342 tons) and *Darling* (150 tons) which made up the flotilla. 'Nothing was spared to make the voyage a success.'

The outcome was the establishment, in 1612, of a 'factory' (trading post) at Surat, in the north-west Indian state of Gujerat.[5] In 1639, another factory was established, at Madras on the Coromandel Coast of south-east India. Here, the Company created a fortified settlement, Fort St George, which in 1644 became the chief administrative location, or 'presidency'.

In the eighteenth century, rivalry between England and France for the control of India came to a head. The British were ultimately successful, when Major-General Robert Clive (1725-1774, 1st Baron Clive), also known as Clive of India, defeated the French at Arcot (Tamil Nadu) in 1751; the Nawab of Bengal at Plassey (Bengal) in 1757, and the Royal Navy established control of the seas. These successes enabled the HEIC to become the effective ruler of a large part of the subcontinent. Furthermore, following the Battle of Baksar in 1764, the HEIC gained control of the taxation revenues of Bengal—India's richest province. A parliamentary committee was now able to report that 'the Company's ships have increased [in number] in thirty years from thirty to ninety', and that 'the tonnage had also expanded'.[6] However, the bubble was shortly to burst.

Famine in Bengal, brought on by drought, lasted from 1769 to 1773. Millions perished and the HEIC was adjudged to have exacerbated the situation by increasing the taxes of agricultural produce and profiteering from the sale of rice and grain. By 1773, for this and other reasons such as mismanagement, corruption, and nepotism, the Company had become not only discredited, but also greatly indebted. Its profits and share price collapsed, whereupon the government passed the Regulating Act, designed to overhaul its management structure. This was followed, in 1784, by the passing of the India Act. A board of control was created, and from henceforth the HEIC would be governed, jointly, by the Company and the Crown.

* * * * *

Although the wreckage of *Halsewell* lies in relatively shallow water, diving on the wreck is no easy task, owing to changing tides, swirling currents, and falls of rock from the adjacent cliff side, which are not only a danger in themselves, but also tend to obscure what remains of the ship. However, many coins have been retrieved, including several Georgian golden guineas, an Indian silver rupee, and many Spanish 'reals'. (It is a fact acknowledged by divers that items made of gold, more so than any other metal, tend, when immersed in sea water to deteriorate the least and in this instance, the golden guineas are in virtually mint condition. The same cannot be said of objects made of iron, which corrodes quickly in saline solution.)

The rupee, which dates from 1775-1785, was issued by the Benares Mint in the district of Benares, Province of Awadh, which was governed by Nawab Viziers. Minted in the name of the Mughal emperor, the coin was probably the personal property of one of the ship's company, obtained on a previous visit to India.[7]

The Spanish silver 'real' was the international currency of the day: the silver from which they were minted having been obtained in Spain's South American colonies. Eight reales were equivalent to one Spanish dollar, hence the colloquial name for reales—'pieces of eight'.

East Indiamen were therefore obliged to carry a considerable quantity of this currency, of which the eight-real piece was perhaps the most popular. However, because such coins were not acceptable currency in the Indian hinterland, an agreement was reached for the HEIC to send its bullion to the Mughal mint in Surat (the majority of the Indian subcontinent being ruled by the Mughal Empire until the early eighteenth century). However, by 1672 the Company had established a mint of its own in Bombay, where coins of copper and tin were manufactured to serve its local needs. In 1717 the Company commenced the minting of silver rupees of Indian style, with inscriptions in accordance with Islamic tradition and in the name of the Mughal emperor.[8]

For those with no prior knowledge of *Halsewell*, one coin in particular which was retrieved, provides an indication that the vessel was employed in the service of the HEIC. This is a gold mohur, minted for the Company (Bengal Presidency) at Murshidbad in the Indian State of Bengal, and dated 1776.[9]

Not only did the Company have its own coinage, it also flew its own flag, featuring, at the time in question, seven horizontal red stripes on a white background, with the British Union flag in the top left-hand corner.

The Honourable Company Ship (HCS) *Halsewell*

HCS *Halsewell*, the subject of this account, made three voyages to the East Indies, the last of which ended tragically, as will be seen. Her history is as follows:

> When a worn-out East Indiaman was decommissioned, this was not the end of the story. She was then dismantled and any sound timbers (e.g. keel, ribbing, etc.) were used in the construction of the new ship, which was built on the so-called 'bottom' of the old one, following a tradition known as 'Hereditary Bottoms'. In this way, precious timber was salvaged and recycled. In the case of *Halsewell*, the vessel which she replaced was her present Captain Peirce's former command, the *Earl of Ashburnham*.[1]
>
> *Halsewell* was built at Greenland Dock, situated on the west bank of the River Thames, opposite the Isle of Dogs and approximately halfway between Rotherhithe and Deptford. Her builders were John and William Wells (whose firm, of the same name, in the fifteen years from 1777 to 1792, launched twenty-one ships for charter by the HEIC).[2]

Halsewell was a three-masted ship with three decks. At 776 tons, and with a length of 139 feet 7 inches, she was armed with 26 cannon in order to protect her valuable cargoes.[3] She was said to be 'one of the finest ships in the service, and supposed to be in the most perfect condition for her [first] voyage...'.[4] She was launched 'off the stocks' (the stocks being a frame used to support a ship out of water when under construction) on 24 August 1778. She then 'warped* down to Deptford', a mile and a half downstream, where she docked.

*To warp is to 'move a ship along by hauling on a rope attached to a stationary object on shore'.[5]

Here, following the erection of her masts, she was rigged, and her crew employed 'bending sails [securing them to the yards] & getting our Bower Anchor [main anchor, one of two which were carried at the ship's bow] to ye Bows'. Spare masts, spars, and cable[6] [rope] were brought aboard, together with her guns and ammunition. Her yards were then blacked and tarred, and her masts scraped and 'payed'—coated with turpentine. She was than provisioned with such items as salted beef and pork, suet, bread, biscuit, flour, cheese, butter, currants and raisins, oatmeal, oats, barley, bran, mustard seed, potatoes, oranges and lemons, butter, peas, red and white herrings, salmon, vinegar, ale, beer, wine, rum, cider, brandy and, of course, water.[7]

Lime juice or lemon juice, sufficient to last the entire crew for the whole voyage was included,[8] for it was known that this was prophylactic against scurvy—characterized by swollen and bleeding gums and the failure of wounds to heal, a disease which particularly affected poorly nourished sailors.[9]

In order that fresh meat and milk be available, routinely, aboard ships of the HEIC

> there was a cow carried, and later on the calf, which was always brought on board with its mother, [and] became veal when the ship had crossed the line and was nearer India. In addition there were also ducks and fowls, sheep and pigs, so that the ship's boats and decks were often mildly suggestive of a farmyard.[10]

The fowls were kept in coops on the decks—a fact which was to have particular significance for two of *Halsewell*'s crew in that ship's time of crisis.

The ship's ballast—'kentledge'—usually took the form of scrap iron or pigs of iron, contained in wooden crates; extra ballast being provided by spare cannon, which were stored in the hold. Prior to sailing, it was essential that this was evenly distributed—or 'levelled'—so that the ship might sail on an 'even keel'. ('A great deal of valuable room had to be wasted in the excessive amount of pig-iron ballast which these ships had to carry'.)[11]

In respect of new recruits to an East Indiaman, its captain 'had strict instructions' to see that they

> ... wore the clothes which the Company provided, and that the men did not sell them for liquor; also that these men did not desert.[12]

Finally, officers from the Honourable Company came aboard to survey the ship before she proceeded to Blackwall, where she 'made fast'—moored.

Here, new recruits were brought aboard and 'private trade' goods (see below) loaded, together with brandy and stores 'for the [expected] Soldiers' (see below). The ship now weighed anchor and set sail; one pilot (a person with expert local knowledge qualified to take charge of a ship entering or leaving confined waters), [13] taking charge of her journey from Blackwall to Gravesend, whereupon another took her from Gravesend to the Isle of Wight. [14]

It was traditional for an East Indiaman to pause at Mother Bank, an important anchorage off the north-east coat of the Isle of Wight, in the Solent across the water from Portsmouth, city and naval port of Hampshire. Here, three directors of the Company would come aboard to survey the ship, having been greeted with a customary thirteen-gun salute, both on their arrival and on their departure. (The firing of gun salutes was an essential part of etiquette. On the anniversary of His Majesty King George III's Accession to the Throne, which had occurred on 25 October 1760, for example, or on His Majesty's birthday, 4 June, a 21-gun salute was the order of the day.)

It was also the custom at the Mother Bank, to take on board contingents of His Majesty's troops for conveyance to India, where they would have the task of guarding the Company's factories. This having been accomplished, the gun deck had to be washed, and the 'Great Guns & Small Arms exercised'. [15]

It was customary for East Indiamen to sail in convoy (often with a Royal Naval escort) for mutual safety and support. However, over the course of a voyage to the East Indies, the number of ships in the convoy often varied, when some joined it and others departed; or as ships were lost due to shipwreck, enemy action, fire, etc., or were delayed.

A 'watch' was a period of duty of four hours duration, 'the seamen being divided into two watches, for the purpose, and the officers into three'. [16] Life for the crew consisted of periods of frenetic activity, alternating with long weeks or months of relative boredom, as the ship plied her way across the oceans, propelled by favourable trade winds.

During their spare time, *Halsewell*'s ordinary seamen—'foremastmen'— would while away their time 'picking Oakhum'—a loose fibre obtained by picking old rope to pieces. This could then be used for caulking—to caulk being to stop up the seams between the ship's planking. This was followed by sealing with molten pitch, thus rendering the timbers watertight. [17]

The crew would also engage themselves in the 'Drawing & Knotting of Yarns'—i.e. extracting threads from old rope and knotting them together for further use, and in 'scraping the masts'—prior to cleaning and greasing them. [18]

'For the Preservation of good Order on board the Company's Ships,' candles in the cabins had to be extinguished by 10 o'clock at the latest. Even before that hour, the utmost precautions had to be taken to prevent any lights from being visible to other ships passing in the night; it was the hallowed custom of East India captains to shorten sail at dusk, and while dawdling through the darkness under easy canvas, the ships were sitting targets for a privateer or pirate.[19]

It was of vital importance that the fabric of the vessel be maintained in good order, especially on a long voyage when a ship was far from home. Periodically, the masts were accordingly scraped and greased; the rigging overhauled and blacked and tarred (treated with a coating of tar to prevent the ropes from rotting); the sails repaired; the sides of the hull re-caulked and the ship painted—the latter task being performed by the gunner. In order for the hull to be scrubbed, caulked, and coated with pitch and tar, it was necessary to 'heel' the ship—i.e. tilt her to first one side and then the other— or to 'hog' the ship—i.e. alter the distribution of ballast in such a way that first the bows, and then the stern rise higher in the water and hence become more exposed.

Attention was paid to cleanliness and hygiene—again vital with so large a number of people being crammed into so small a space. It was customary, for example, to wash the gun deck and the orlop (referred to by Captain Peirce as 'Hollop') deck—this being the lowest deck of the ship—with vinegar, and then fumigate them with burning tobacco or charcoal. Discipline was strictly enforced, misdemeanours being punished by flogging.

> This punishment was inflicted over the bare back by the brawny boatswain's mate armed with the cat-o'-nine-tails, [a rope whip with nine knotted lashes], the victim being triced up by the thumbs. And when it was all over, a bucket of salt water washed the blood away.[20]

It was usual for an East Indiaman to carry fee-paying passengers, perhaps a dozen or so, and for them, it was a different story. For them, card games such as whist and backgammon, and also chess were favourite pastimes. In fact, a number of chess pieces were recovered from the wreck.

> On Saturday nights there would be songs and dancing. No work was allowed to be performed on Sunday except what was necessary, though manuscript journals rather show that this regulation was not much respected. The crew were mustered in their best clothes, and then everyone that could be spared was present at prayers.[21]

Those passengers fortunate enough to be invited to dine at the captain's table might expect to partake of a dinner of pea soup, roast leg of mutton, hogs' pudding, two fowls, two hams, two ducks, corned round of beef, mutton pies, pork pies, mutton chops, stewed cabbage and potatoes; followed by 'an enormous plum pudding and washed down with porter, spruce beer, port wine, sherry, gin, rum etc'.[22]

Go on board of an Indiaman, count over the servants, the cooks, the musicians; behold the feasting and attendants! Listen to the symphonies, and tell me sincerely, whether it would not rather impress you with an idea of Cleopatra sailing down the Cydnus to meet Mark Anthony, than a rough Captain venturing across immense oceans, and defying their storms and hidden rocks, to import the merchandise of India?[23]

*   *   *   *   *

Fragments of the ship's bell have been recovered from the wreckage, one of which is embossed with the number '1': this presumably being part of the number '1778' the year in which she was launched. Also recovered were portions of her rudder-hinging mechanism. This consisted of a series of gudgeons which were bolted at intervals to the hull by means of two arms, shaped to fit around the sternpost (extension of the keel aft), and pintles which were bolted to the rudder. Each pintle was fitted with a downward-pointing pin which fitted into a ring on the gudgeon, thus forming a hinge.[24]

3

The Allure of the East

What made it financially worthwhile for the HEIC to send its ships halfway around the world, in order to trade with the East? Early letters, sent home to the Company by its emissaries ('servants') in the East Indies, provide valuable information as to the type of goods which, when exported, might 'attract the people of the East Indies' and likewise, of the type of 'produce that could be sent to England in return'.[1] One such letter, written in 1609, nine years after the Company had been created, describes Agra on the River Jumna in northern India, as

> … a very great Citie and populous, built with stone, having faire and large streets, with a faire River running by it, which falleth into the Gulfe of Bengala [Bengal]. Hither is great resort of Merchants from Persia, and out of India, and very much merchandize of Silks, and cloths and of precious stones both [Rubies], Diamonds, and Pearles. The Diamonds are found in diverse places, as in Bisnagar ['Visnagar', Gujarat], in [Delhi] and here in Agra. But Rubyes, Saphyres and Spinels [gemstones of variable colour and consisting chiefly of magnesium and aluminium oxides] are found in Pegu.
>
> Bramy [Brahmapur, Bengal] is the cheifest place for Indico ['indigo'—a dark blue dye obtained from the indigo plant],[2] in all the East India, where are twelve Indico milles. It groweth on small bushes, and beareth a seede like a Cabbage seede. Being cut downe, it lyeth on heapes for halfe a [year] to rot, and then by Oxen it is troden out from the stalkes, and afterward is ground very fine and then boiled in furnaces, and so sorted out into severall sorts. The best Indico is there worth eightpence a pound....[3]

Another letter, received by the Company on 30 August of that same year from Surat, from another of its servants describes how

Cotton wool may here be had [in] what quantity your Worship (presumably the chairman of the Company) shall desire.... There is an excellent linen made at Cape Comore [the southernmost point of India].

Also to be obtained was 'large pepper'; 'gum lack' (a resinous substance produced by lac insects and used as sealing wax or varnish); 'myrrh, rice, green ginger, and Opium in great abundance...'. Exotic birds and beasts, which were purchased on behalf of the Company and supplied to its patrons, were also considered valuable merchandise.

Tea, however, was the principal product which the Company's ships carried homeward from the East, and 'it was always reckoned that an 800-ton ship would be able to bring home about 750,000 lb' of that commodity.[4] In the latter part of the eighteenth century, an estimated 12 million tons was imported into Britain annually, of which a large proportion was smuggled, there being a tax on the product.

Tea is generally bought from China... of this famous leaf there are divers sorts (though all of one shape) some much better than other, the upper Leaves excelling the others in fineness... which Leaves they gather every day, and drying them in the shade, or in Iron pans over a gentle fire till the humidity be exhausted, they put up close in Leaden Pots, preserve them for their Drink Tea [or 'cha', in Mandarin Chinese] which is used at Meals, and upon all Visits and Entertainment in private Families, and in the Palaces of Grandees.... The said Leaf is of such known verities, that those very Nations so famous for Antiquity, Knowledge and Wisdom, do frequently sell it among themselves for twice its weight in Silver....

It maketh the Body active and lusty... It overcometh superfluous Sleep, and prevents Sleepiness in general, a draught of the Infusion being taken, so that without trouble whole nights may be spent in study without hurt to the Body, in that it moderately heateth and bindeth the mouth of the Stomack... And that the Virtues and Excellencies of this Leaf and Drink are many and great, is evident and manifest by the high esteem and use of it among the [physicians] and knowing men in France, Italy, Holland and other parts of Christendom; and in England it hath been sold in the leaf for six pounds and sometimes for ten pounds the pound weight....[5]

Who could resist such a tempting proposition, provided of course that he or she could afford it? In May 1664, diarist and writer John Evelyn (1620-1706), was truly dazzled by Chinese 'rarities' brought to London by a returned East Indiaman. They included

glorious vests, wrought and embroidered on cloth of gold, but with such lively colours, that for splendour and vividness we have nothing in Europe that approaches it; a girdle studded with agates and rubies of great value and size; knives, of so keen an edge as one could not touch them...; fans like our ladies use, but much larger and with long handles, curiously carved and filled with Chinese characters...[6]

Admiralty official Samuel Pepys (1633-1703), kept a diary in which he included details of his life as a naval administrator, together with juicy details of his personal life, and of intrigues at the Royal Court. Pepys was equally dazzled by the cargo of an East Indiaman, which he inspected in London in November 1665 in company with Lord Brouncker (mathematician and first President of the Royal Society) and Sir Edmond Pooly (Member of Parliament), who

> carried me down into the hold of the India ship, and there did show me the greatest wealth lie in confusion that a man can see in the world. Pepper scattered through every chink, you trod upon it; and in cloves and nutmegs I walked above the knees; whole rooms full, and silk in bales, and boxes of copper-plate*, one of which I saw opened.[7]

*It is likely that this copper plate was for export, not import.

Also to be obtained in the East Indies was 'gum Benjamin' (gum resin, used especially in treating skin irritation), olibanum (frankincense), aloes, sandal (oil of sandal-wood), mace, sugar, and ginger. Not for nothing would poet William Cowper, refer to 'India's spicy shores'; poet Edward Gibbon, to 'the treasures of India', and that country be described as the 'jewel in the crown' of the British Empire!

Trade was, of course, a two way process, and according to the Company's early traders, products suitable for export from Britain to the East Indies included

> cloth, of all kinds of light and pleasant colours pleasing to the eye, as Venice reds [Venetian red—a pigment, dark scarlet in colour and derived from ferric oxide], stamels [stamel—a type of woollen cloth, or of the garment made from it, which was typically dyed red], some few scarlets [scarlet coloured clothes] for presents and also to sell to great men, Poppinjay greens of the brightest dye, cinnamon colours, light dove colours, peach colours, silver colours, light yellows and with others like, but no dark or sad colours for they are not here vendible.... Quicksilver [mercury], some 50 or 63 Kintals would be sold [for] about 4 or 5 m. per seer.* Red Coral reasonable large and fair unwrought are very good commodity....

*One kintal equals 100 pounds in weight; 'm'—maund—was a unit of currency, the 'small maund' being equivalent to £27 and the 'great maund' to £32½; seer—a traditional unit of weight in India and South Asia, of approximately 11 ounces]. Red Coral reasonable large and fair unwrought are very good commodity....

> Of new drinking glasses, trenchers [wooden plates or platters] for sweetmeats, but especially looking glasses [i.e. mirrors] of all sorts and different prices (but not small baubles) some reasonable quantity would be sold to good profit and I verily suppose that some fair large looking glass would be highly accepted by this King [the Mughal Emperor Jahangir], for he effects not the value of anything but rarity in everything, inasmuch that some pretty new fangled toys would give him high content, though their value were small, for he wants no worldly wealth or riches, possessing an inestimable treasury and is, it is thought, herein far exceeding the great Turk [Ottoman Emperor]....[8]

In addition, leatherware, and in particular saddlery and the finest London-made boots and shoes, 'always yielded a hundred per cent [profit] in Bengal'.[9]

Captain Richard Peirce, Commander of *Halsewell*

The East Indiaman *Halsewell* made three voyages to the East Indies, including her last, fateful one in 1786. On each occasion she was commanded by Captain Richard Peirce. Peirce's parents, his namesake Captain Richard Peirce and Ann Peirce née Shiers, were residents of Calcutta (capital city of the Indian state of Bengal), where the HEIC had a fortified station—Fort William. Richard senior and Ann were married in Calcutta on 16 July 1730,[1] and their son Richard, was born in 1736.[2] A year later, in 1737, the city experienced a great earthquake, which caused the steeple of the Church of St Anne to collapse.

Peirce's career with the HEIC commenced in the year 1761 when, at the age of 25 (and having relocated to England), he became Third Mate aboard the HCS *Horsenden* (499 tons), which embarked on a voyage to China. In 1764 he became Second Mate aboard the *Pacific* (499 tons), for a voyage to 'Coast & Bay' (a reference to the Coromandel Coast of South-east India and the Bay of Bengal).

On 25 September 1767, Peirce was married at London's Church of St Dunstan-in-the-East to Mary, daughter of Thomas Burston Esquire, Collector of Customs for the County of Surrey and co-owner/manager (or 'husband') with banker Peter Esdaile Esquire of *Halsewell*.[3] The newly-wedded couple set up home at Kingston-upon-Thames in Surrey. They would produce 9 (surviving) children: 2 sons and 7 daughters.[4]

Meanwhile, the following year, 1768, Peirce was appointed captain of the East Indiaman *Earl of Ashburnham* (499 tons), for a voyage to Coast and China, which was repeated in 1772. Finally, in 1778, Peirce, described as a man 'of distinguished ability and exemplary character',[5] was appointed captain of *Halsewell*.

Commands of East Indiamen were invariably sold, by the owner of the ship, for a sum of between £6,000 and £12,000 (provided, of course, that the new commander had the approval of the Company). In this instance, it was Peirce's father-in-law who was co-owner of *Halsewell*, and therefore it is likely that the command was granted to him on the most favourable of terms. In regard to a commander's uniform, the Company's specifications were as follows.

> Fine blue Coat, black Genoa Velvet round the Cuffs.... Black Velvet Lapells.... Black Velvet panteen Cape [with] straight Flaps....[6] The fore Parts lined with Buff silk serge, Back slit and turns faced with the same. One Button on each hip, and one at the bottom; Gold embroidered Button Holes throughout and gilt Buttons, with the Company's Crest.[7]

One may therefore imagine *Halsewell*'s captain, cutting a fine figure as he bestrode the quarterdeck, resplendent in his fine uniform, including cream-coloured waistcoat, cravat, knee-breeches, stockings, buttoned shoes, and tricorn hat.

*   *   *   *   *

A button retrieved from the wreck bears the Company's crest—a rampant lion holding a crown between its paws, in an oval border lined with rope twist. This came from the uniform of one of the ship's officers, possibly from the coatee (short, close-fitting coat) of Captain Peirce himself, and would originally have been gilded.[8]

*   *   *   *   *

The roundhouse was situated on the after part of the quarterdeck, immediately forward of which was the cuddy, which comprised the captain's stateroom, including his bedchamber on one side of the ship, and the dining room on the other.[9] The cuddy's glass doors provided direct access to the quarterdeck.

> Only the high-ranking passengers, those occupying the expensive accommodations in the roundhouse and great cabin, dined in the cuddy with the captain and his leading officers.[10]

Commanders of HEIC ships were paid a nominal salary of £10 per month; their main remuneration deriving from other sources.[11] For example, a captain enjoyed the privilege of 'private trade', whereby the Company

Captain Richard Peirce. Photo: *New London Magazine*.

permitted him to utilize a portion of the ship's hold for his own private cargo. Such cargo, provided that the captain had invested wisely, could be sold in the East for a profit of several thousand pounds. (On more than one occasion, the captain of an East Indiaman had included a pack of English foxhounds in his private trade!)

For the outward journey, the tonnage allowance for such private trade, as stipulated by the Company, was on a steeply sliding scale: for the captain, 56 tons; for the First Mate, 8 tons; for the Second Mate, 6 tons; for the surgeon, 6 tons, for the purser, 3 tons, and so forth down as far as the cooper, armourer, and sailmaker. For the homeward journey, privileges were somewhat less generous. Furthermore, if the captain and his officers were unable to invest up to the full amount of their allowances, they were permitted to make up the deficit in bullion, again on a sliding scale of £3,000's worth for the captain, £300 for the First Mate, etc.[12] Therefore, every crew member, with the exception of the seamen had a stake in the enterprise and a vested interest in making the voyage a success.

Also, captains were permitted to charge a fee for the carrying of passengers, on a scale laid down by the Company, and not to exceed the following amounts: 'general [presumably army] officers', £250; 'Gentlemen of the Council [i.e. members of the Company's provincial councils in India] or colonels', £200; majors and senior merchants, £150; writers, £110; subalterns (British Army officers below the rank of captain), £110; assistant surgeons and cadets, each £95.[13]

> The commanders' income from passengers, negligible in the early days, increased appreciably as thriving towns grew up around the forts at Madras, Bombay and Calcutta and the Company's control in Bengal spread, necessitating a flood of administrators, lawyers, military officers, officials of every kind, not to speak of the ladies, wives and children who followed them.[14]
>
> Another perquisite came from the large fees wealthy influential people were prepared to give to the commander to secure midshipmen's places for their sons or protégés, places which were in great demand as the first rung of the ladder which would probably lead to an eventual fortune.[15]

A single voyage could therefore net a commander such as Captain Peirce, a profit of between £8,000 and £10,000, and possibly as much as £30,000.[16]

Halsewell's First Voyage (1778-1781): An Unpleasant Encounter with Horatio Nelson

Halsewell set sail from Gravesend on Tuesday 1 December 1778 for Coast and China (or, to be more accurate, to Coast, Bay, and China). Her cargo was principally copper, but also lead, and, of course, items being shipped for 'private trade'. The voyage would take her to Madeira (North Atlantic); Island of Gorée (Senegal); Table Bay (South Africa); Madras (India); Whampoa Island (Pearl river delta, China); Landrone Islands (Pacific Ocean); Carimata Strait (between the west coast of Borneo and the Island of Billiton); the Straits of Bali, and home via St Helena (South Atlantic)—a total distance of about 35,000 miles.

In addition to her normal complement she carried a detachment of His Majesty's 73rd [Highland] Regiment of Foot, namely a captain, two lieutenants, one ensign, 89 non-commissioned officers, five women, and two children.[1]

It was normal practice for the captain of an East Indiaman to keep a daily record of each voyage embarked upon, and having completed his logbook, sign it personally. Captain Peirce was no exception. He referred to the log as his *Journal*, and signed his name 'Rd Peirce'. (Here, it should be noted that in virtually all other sources, an incorrect spelling, i.e. 'Pierce' is used. Therefore, for present purposes, the two spellings are regarded as synonymous.)

In his logbook, Captain Peirce kept meticulous records of data such as latitude, longitude, distance travelled, and barometric pressure. It was of vital importance to know the ship's position at any one time, either by using landmarks or astronomical observations; or by dead reckoning, the calculation being made from her direction of travel and distance travelled, measured by log-line. The apparatus for this consisted of a float attached to a knotted line that was wound on a reel; the distance run out in a certain time being used as an estimate of the vessel's speed. In the logbook was also entered a wealth of information about the conditions which pertained aboard ship, relating, for example, to passengers, goods carried, discipline, and the maintenance of the vessel.

At Madeira on 12 April 1779, seamen Andrew Stewart and John Duncan, each received two dozen lashes for mutiny, and at the same time Thomas Grundy for 'going on shore & wanting to leave the ship'. The men were 'put in irons' (i.e. fettered), until an opportunity came 'to send them on board the Admiral'—i.e. the Royal Naval Admiral's flagship, where they would doubtless be 'pressed'—i.e. forcibly enlisted into service with the Royal Navy). Jacob Archer, one of the Company's recruits (new hands), was punished with a dozen lashes for theft. Others were more fortunate. Two seamen were 'put in irons... for refusing to do their duty', but later released on 'promising Good behaviour'.

On 7 May, a seemingly trivial entry appeared in the logbook, Captain Peirce having recorded the presence of 'Several Swallows & other small Birds about [the] Ship'. But as every mariner knows, such an occurrence invariably indicates that land—in this instance the Island of Goree, Senegal, is not far off.

In that same month, the hazards attendant upon such voyages were illustrated only too graphically, when on 19 May, seaman John Golts 'Fell overboard from the Main Shrouds', whereupon the 'Jolly Boat' (a clinker-built ship's boat, typically situated at the stern of the ship,[2] and used principally to ferry personnel to and fro) was immediately lowered and a search made for him, but without success.

As previously mentioned, it was customary for safety reasons for East Indiamen to sail in convoy, preferably with a Royal Naval escort, and when *Halsewell* weighed anchor on 5 November 1779 and sailed from the Cape of Good Hope, she was in company with no less than six men-of-war (the flagship HMS *Superb*, together with *Exeter*, *Belleisle*, *Burford*, *Worcester*, and *Eagle*), the sloop *Nymph*, and thirteen fellow East Indiamen—namely *Hawke*, *Granby*, *Walpole*, *Ceres*, *Earl of Sandwich*, *Earl of Oxford*, *Duke of Grafton*, *Resolution*, *Princess Royal*, *True Briton*, *Fox*, *Atlas*, and *Norfolk*.

On 22 December, a joyous event occurred on board ship when Ann Lane, wife of one of the private soldiers, 'was [brought] to bed [i.e. delivered] of a female Child'.

On 18 January 1780, *Halsewell* arrived in the 'Madras Road',—a road, or roadstead being a sheltered or partially sheltered stretch of water near to a shore in which vessels might safely ride at anchor. Here, the following day, the 1st Lieutenant of his Majesty's ship *Belleisle*, came aboard '& pressed fifteen of our People'. ('People' was the word used by Captain Peirce to describe his crewmen).

Courses	K	F	Winds &c.	Wednesday, the 24th day of November
SE –	3	5	NE	Hazey — Fresh Breezes & Hazey Weath
	4	4		with small Rain
	5	..		
	5	..	Cloudy	
	5	3	Ins.t Reefs	A Large Swell & the Ship rowls
	5	3	Squally –	very deep —
	5	5		
	5	5		
	5	..		
	5	2		
	6	2	Do	The Ceres missing in the Morn
	6	4	Small Rain	from ye Fleet – ye Hawk far a
	6	3	Do	head with her Fore topmast g.
	6	2	2.do –	
	5	5	NNE Shortd Sail	Barometer PM–29.6
ENE –	4	2	Found Missing on of ye Fleet.	Moon 29.5
SEbE –	5	5	SEbEr. In 2nd R. Hand Slig. nor. St.	
SE.	5	5	WbW. In 3d R. F St. Hand MSt.	
	5	4		No Observation
	4	3		
Pr Log	131	Miles		

Course	D	8	E	MD	Dep	X Lo.	Lo. in	Bearing & Dist.r
S4½S	130	39	124	27.25	36.52	154	52.24	

Halsewell: extract from logbook, 24 November 1779.

This is my Original Journal Part 1st.

Witness
R Cole

R Peirce

Captain Peirce's signature, from *Halsewell*'s log book.

On 20 July seaman Joseph Thomas, 'was Drowned in going to Swim while ye Long Boat was on Shore at ye. Island'. In addition to the possibility of such accidents befalling the crew, there was also the possibility of epidemics of sickness breaking out aboard the vessel. On this voyage, for example, several more crewmen died at sea, including gunner's servant Thomas Pewter, and Frederick Whieland, servant to the Second Mate.

On Christmas Day 1780, in company with fellow East Indiamen *Granby*, *Earl of Oxford*, *Earl of Sandwich*, *Britannia*, and the country ship *Favourite*, *Halsewell* set sail from Whampoa Island, situated in China's Pearl River delta to the south of Canton. ('Country ships' were those which plied between the ports of the East Indies, engaged in 'country trade'—private enterprise, legitimately engaged in by the Company's employees.) A week later, on 1 January 1781, Captain Peirce wrote in his logbook, 'I take my Departure from the Ladrone [an archipelago of 104 islands, situated south of the mouth of the Pearl river]...'.[3] However, extricating the ship from the estuary proved to be no easy matter, owing to the shallowness of the water. The longboat—a sailing ship's largest boat[4] was therefore sent ahead night and day, for several days, to keep 'a good look out' and perform soundings every hour, and sometimes every half hour, of the depth beneath the ship's hull, until finally *Halsewell* reached the safety of the Carimata Passage—i.e. strait between Borneo and Sumatra.

*   *   *   *   *

Soundings were taken using a lead sounding-weight, which was attached a long length of rope—'line'—marked off at regular intervals with bunting of different colours to indicate different depths. The small cavity at the lower end of the weight was filled with tallow—a solid substance made from rendered animal fat—which adhered to the material on the sea bed, thus giving an indication of its nature. Such a sounding weight was retrieved from the wreck of *Halsewell*.

A considerable quantity of munitions have also been recovered over the years. Professor Robin Pingree of Southampton University's Oceanography Department and his team, for example, retrieved a dozen or so 9-pound cannon balls and about the same number of 6.5-pound cannon balls, together with two grenades (small bombs, thrown by hand or launched mechanically).[5] Another cannon ball, this one encrusted with grapeshot, was discovered by Ian Carruthers. Pingree's colleague, Wally Hammond, developed a technique for preserving such iron objects, which were otherwise liable quickly to corrode away to dust, by immersing them in a saturated solution of sodium carbonate and subjecting it to electrolysis. As for the grenades, said Hammond, when their internal residue was examined by mass spectrometer, it was found to consist of carbon and sulphur. This is not surprising since charcoal—a source of carbon—and sulphur are both constituents of gunpowder.[6]

Quilted grapeshot, an example of which was also recovered, consisted of balls of grapeshot, held together by netting made of twine. This was attached to a metal stem, which emanated from the centre of a metal plate, which in turn was mounted on a circular wooden disc, specially designed to fit snugly into the barrel of the cannon. Quilted shot was highly effective when used against massed ranks of enemy personnel.

The question is, were any of *Halsewell*'s guns ever fired in anger? To this, the answer is no, as far as is known. However, she herself *was fired upon*, on one memorable occasion, not by the enemy but, paradoxically, by a vessel of His Majesty's Royal Navy, as will now be seen!

On 12 October 1781, more than two and a half years after she had set sail from England, the Scilly Isles came into view: a sight which must have gladdened the hearts of her ship's company. As the ship sailed up Channel, there were further familiar sights to be seen: the Lizard, South Cornwall; the Eddystone (rocks and lighthouse); Start Point, Devonshire; Portland Bill, Dorsetshire; Isle of Wight; Beachy Head, Sussex and the proverbial white cliffs of Dover; and finally, South Foreland and Margate, Kent.

At midday on 28 October, *Halsewell* was lying at anchor at the buoy of the Mouse, at the mouth of the Thames estuary off Shoeburyness, Essex. Within a few hours her crewmen would set foot, once again, on England's shores, or so they hoped. However, Captain Peirce and his ship's company were to receive a rude awakening, for, as he himself recorded in his ship's logbook

> At Noon came on board 2 of his Majesty's Lieutenants to impress [or 'press'—i.e. force to serve in the Royal Navy] our Men which they resisted & Arm'd to defend themselves.

At 5 p.m., ignoring these attempts by the Royal Navy to purloin his crewmen, Captain Peirce weighed anchor. However, shortly after 9 p.m., *Halsewell* 'was Fir'd at by several Ships [i.e. of the Royal Navy]', but Peirce 'could not bring our Ship too [i.e. to a halt], the People refusing to blow the sails up or let go the Anchor'. Whereupon

> His Majesty's Frigate *Albermarle* [28-guns, commanded by] Capn. Nelson kept firing Shot at us one of which struck off the Thick [presumably thickest part] of the Main Mast [and] another [passed] through the Main Course [the largest of the sails].

Subsequently, there 'came on board Capn. Nelson with offers to our People which they all refused'. This was none other than Horatio Nelson himself.

Born in 1758, Nelson, at the age of only 20, was given command of his first ship. On 15 August of the present year, 1781, he had taken command of HMS *Albermarle*, and on 23 October, was instructed to collect an inbound convoy of the Russian Company (an English trading company, otherwise known as the Muscovy Company) at Elsenor, island of Zealand (eastern Denmark) and escort it back to Britain. Nelson was aware that the three ships of his present fleet were seriously undermanned, so when he learnt that several homeward-bound East Indiamen were shortly to arrive in the Thames Estuary (one of which was *Halsewell*), this presented him with the opportunity he was looking for.

On the morning of the following day, 29 October, Captain Nelson again came aboard *Halsewell* and 'told the People if they refused serving his Majesty, he must bring the Frigate alongside'. The outcome was that the entire ship's crew was pressed, and only Captain Peirce and his officers, together with 'the Foreigners and Servants', and presumably any private passengers, remained aboard. (It is likely that 'foreigners' was a reference to lascars—i.e. sailors from the East Indies, recruited by the Company as crew for homeward-bound vessels, subsequently to be returned to the East as passengers—and that 'servants' referred to the personal servants of the captain and important passengers.) However, Nelson did graciously condescend to supply a lieutenant and twenty-four of his own men to 'work the Ship [*Halsewell*] up to her Moorings'.

Twenty-four years later, as Vice-Admiral of the British Fleet aboard his flagship HMS *Victory*, Nelson would destroy a combined Franco-Spanish fleet at the Battle of Trafalgar (21 October 1805), during the course of which he would be fatally wounded.

Meanwhile, the thoughts of the impressed crewmen can only be imagined. Having been away from home for almost three years, they were now denied the chance to be reunited with their loved ones, and instead, faced the prospect of spending further long years at sea, under the harsh discipline of the Royal Navy.

Halsewell having returned to Blackwall on 3 November 1781, Captain Dampier came aboard to open her hatches,[7] which had presumably been sealed for security reasons to protect against looters. It took almost three months to unload her cargo, which included 800 chests of Bohea tea, grown in the Wuyi Mountains of south-east China; the same quantity of Congo tea (or 'Congou')—a high quality tea grown in the Fujian region of south-east China, and of Singlo, another type of Chinese tea; sago; silks; china (some as private trade), and lead, together with 'Private Trade Wine'.[8]

In that same year, Captain Peirce and his wife Mary and family relocated to Walnut Tree House, Kingston-upon-Thames—a mansion set in the grounds of a large estate, which reflected the wealth and status of its owner.

Halsewell's Second Voyage (1782-1784): An Important Passenger

As already mentioned, it was not unusual for a seaman who had signed on for the duration of a voyage to have a sudden change of mind. When *Halsewell* was about to embark on her second voyage, for example

James Hopper, one of the Honble. Companys Recruits, by which his Shoes being found in the Head [bows] [is] Imagine[d] to have gone Overboard.

And when, on Christmas Day, *Halsewell* lay at anchor in the lower part of the Hope (a creek situated near to the mouth of the River Thames in the Parish of Stanford-le-Hope), Daniel McNeal, another of the Company's recruits, was found to be missing, having apparently made his escape by swimming ashore.

Halsewell set sail from Gravesend on 24 December 1782 for Coast and Bay, in company with HCS *Fox* and HCS *Atlas*. This time, the voyage would take her to Cape Verde (archipelago in the Atlantic Ocean, 350 miles west of Senegal); Johanna Island (Indian Ocean—part of Comoros archipelago, located off the eastern coast of Africa in the Mozambique Channel); Madras (India); Kedgeree (Bay of Bengal, India), and St Helena (South Atlantic), a total distance of about 35,000 miles.

To her normal complement was added an officer and 59 private soldiers of His Majesty's 83rd Regiment, and two officers and 78 privates of His Majesty's 36th Regiment, together with two women—presumably the wives of soldiers—together with their baggage and bedding. Her cargo consisted principally of copper, and also lead, 'bales of small arms', 'rod iron, and iron chains', and 'some brass ordnance'. Also among the items loaded, prior to *Halsewell*'s sailing, was a viol (a stringed instrument of mediaeval origin, played with a bow), doubtless to be used by a musician for the entertainment of the officers and passengers. The most notable of these passengers was the artist Johann Zoffany. It was said of Captain Peirce that

added to his other qualifications, [he] had great taste in the polite arts. He was the means of making the fortune of Mr. Zoffany the painter by taking him to India, and recommending him there.[1]

Johann Zoffany was born at Ratisbon, Bavaria in 1733, the son of an architect. At the age of 13 he ran away to Italy, where he stayed for twelve years. In 1758, he

migrated to England, where at first he seems to have been reduced to great straits. He was starving in a garret in [London's] Drury Lane when... he was made known to Stephen Rimbault, the clock-maker, of Great St. Andrew Street, Seven Dials [Covent Garden], at that time noted for his twelve-tuned Dutch clocks. Rimbault gave young Zoffany immediate employment upon his clock-faces, which it was his practice to ornament with landscapes and moving figures. From Rimbault Zoffany passed into the services of [painter] Benjamin Wilson, as drapery painter and assistant....

Such was Zoffany's rise to fame and fortune that he came to enjoy the patronage of royalty. In 1769 he was nominated a member of The Royal Academy, and the following year, at the Frith Street Gallery, Soho, he exhibited a portrait of King George III, his Queen and family.

He left England in 1772, assisted by a present of 300l. [pounds] and an introduction from the king to the grand duke of Tuscany. In 1778 he travelled to Vienna, in order to present the Empress, Maria Theresa [Holy Roman Empress, Archduchess of Austria, and Queen of Hungary and Bohemia] with a portrait of the Royal Family of Tuscany, which she had commissioned from him.

He had been seven years in Italy when he reached England again in 1779. For some time he worked assiduously at his profession. Then in 1783 from unrest or cupidity he suddenly determined to start for India.

(It is likely that Zoffany boarded *Halsewell* as she lay at the Mother Bank, prior to her departure from there on 4 March 1783. His mission was evidently successful, for it was subsequently reported that in India 'he received many lucrative commissions' and 'returned to England once more in 1790, a richer man'.)[2]

In Maidstone Museum & Art Gallery's collection of love tokens, amassed by the Reverend R. W. H. Acworth (1870-1951), is to be found one crafted from a Spanish real, dedicated to 'C. Webster', and dated 1784. On the reverse are the words 'Success to the Halsewell' and a depiction of the ship. (A love token was a gift, usually from a lover or a family member.) Webster does not appear in the list of officers. He was therefore probably an ordinary seaman.

A 'strong gale with a very large, heavy sea, together with 'rain & very sick weather' was encountered in the English Channel. On 29 March 1783, the Cape Verde Island of Bonavista came into view, and the following day, *Halsewell* sailed into Praya Bay. On 2 April, eight of her crew were punished for 'behaving in mutinous manner & attempting to take the Boatswain out of his cabin to ill use him'. On 31 March, *Halsewell* resumed he voyage, in company with HCS *Bellmont* and HCS *Walpole*.

On 14 April, Captain Peirce recorded in his logbook, 'caught a Land Bird something like a Jay but with a green head & breast'. On 27 April, Seaman John Lovell fell overboard. His body was retrieved, but was 'insensible from a blow on his head received on falling.' He 'departed this life' and the following day his body was committed to the deep, with the usual ceremony.

Throughout the latter part of May, 'fresh', 'strong', and 'moderate' gales were encountered. On 9 June, two Seamen were punished with a dozen lashes for 'cutting canvas, out of one of the ship's sails' and for 'taking canvas off the Quarter Deck'.

On 17 June, *Halsewell* having rounded the Cape of Good Hope, the Island of Madagascar came in sight, and on 23rd, she anchored off the Island of Johanna, and fresh water was taken aboard, together with livestock.

On 26 July, *Halsewell* arrived at Madras. Here, the soldiers disembarked, together with their baggage; the Company's cargo was unloaded; the ship was re-provisioned, and fresh water taken aboard. On 25 August, she set sail for Bengal.

On 4 September, *Halsewell* arrived at Kedgeree. Here private trade was delivered, and copper unloaded. Then, a vast quantity of bales of cotton were loaded, together with several hundred bags of saltpetre (a constituent of gunpowder), and redwood (sappanwood, from which a red dye used to dye fabrics is obtained). Meanwhile, Captain Peirce and the passengers paid a visit to Calcutta. On 17 October, *Halsewell* was hogged, 10 caulkers being employed to 'pay'—i.e. coat her hull with pitch and tar. On 3 February 1784, *Halsewell*, in company with HCS *Ceres* and HCS *Talbot*, set sail for England.

On several occasions during the return journey, 'a strange sail' was observed—always a cause for anxiety, in case it belonged to an enemy vessel. On 25 March, Captain Peirce wrote in his logbook, 'The ships keeping so wide makes me fearful of separation'. He therefore made the signal 'for the ships to close more in my wake'. However, despite this, *Talbot* continued to lag behind.

At sunset on 27 April, the coast of Africa was sighted. On 4 May, Captain Peirce reported 'A Strong Gale with a Mountainous Swell', which caused the ship to 'labour much'.

On 5 May 1784 land was again sighted, and the following day, a sounding was taken at 55 fathoms the result being 'Coarse Sand Small red Stones & broken shells—by these soundings we must be well on the bank.' This was a reference to the Agulhas sandbank, which lies off the Cape of Good Hope and stretches for about 500 miles east to west, and is about 100 miles wide. Having safely negotiated the Cape, *Halsewell* anchored briefly in False Bay, prior to resuming her voyage.

On 7 June, *Halsewell* arrived at the Island of St Helena and duly 'saluted the Fort with 9 Guns'. Here water was taken aboard and stores unloaded. Ten days later, noted Captain Peirce, 'I take my Departure at 2 p.m.'. This was in company with the HCS *Ceres* and HCS *Talbot*. On the homeward voyage the ship was assisted by 'strong', 'fresh' trade winds. On 20 August, HMS *Renown*, from the Island of St Kitts bound for Bristol, joined the convoy.

On 26 August, the Cornish coast was sighted and finally, on 4 September, *Halsewell* arrived at Deptford where, over the course of the next five weeks, her huge cargo of cotton bales and saltpetre was unloaded, together with her private trade.

Inevitably, neither the ship nor her company, nor her companion ships returned from the voyage unscathed. For example, *en route* to Cape Verde, it was reported that 'a heavy and sudden squall [had] carried away the Fore topmast'; at Calcutta, no less than '23 sick people'—i.e. from the ship's company, were hospitalized; on passage home from St Helena, her companion ship HCS *Fox* sustained 'considerable damage … on a rock'.

Also, there were to be many fatalities amongst her crew during the voyage, including that of the Third Mate, ship's surgeon Charles Bromfield, quarter master, armourer, boatswain's servant, carpenter's mate, seven seamen, and two 'landsmen' (a reference, presumably, to new recruits, with no previous experience at sea).[3]

Halsewell's Third Voyage (1786-): Her Officers, Crew, and Passengers

Halsewell's officers, who sailed with her in what was to be her final voyage, were described as 'men of unquestioned knowledge in their profession, and of approved fidelity'[1] to the Company. First Mate (Officer) was Thomas Burston, brother of Captain Peirce's wife Mary, whose career with the Company had begun in 1772, when he had sailed in HCS *Earl of Ashburnham* under Captain Peirce, as captain's servant. Having subsequently served as midshipman aboard HCS *True Briton* and HCS *Royal Henry*, he served once again under Captain Peirce, as Third Mate aboard *Halsewell* on her first aforementioned voyage to the East Indies. On *Halsewell*'s second voyage, he had served as First Mate, it being a requirement of the Company that

> ... a Chief [i.e. First] Mate shall have attained full age of twenty-three years, and have performed a voyage to and from India or China, in the Company's service, in the station of Second or Third Mate.[2]

In other words, where promotion was concerned, the Company operated a hierarchical system, based on previous experience. Now, Burston was to sail, once again, aboard *Halsewell* in the same capacity, on a voyage which would test his strength of character to its very limits.

*   *   *   *   *

The uniform of the First Mate differed from that of the captain in that one small button was to be displayed on each cuff (and for the Second Mate, two small buttons on each cuff, and so forth).[3] One of the many buttons to be recovered from the wreck bore the inscription 'TB'. Clearly, therefore, it had once belonged to Burston himself, and was probably attached to coat.

*   *   *   *   *

Second Mate was Henry Meriton, who had served a seven-year apprenticeship in the Company's West Indian trade as gunner, Second Mate, First Mate, and finally, Master of HCS *John & Richard*. He subsequently served aboard HCS *Pigot* as Third Mate, and finally aboard HCS *Bridgwater* as First Mate. Meriton would play a key role in the drama which was shortly to unfold.

> Third Mate John Rogers, had served his apprenticeship in the Company's Mediterranean, West Indian, and Canadian and Dunkirk trades. In 1782 he joined Pigot as Fourth Mate. Meriton paid tribute to the 'very particular friendship [which] subsisted between himself and Mr. Rogers'; the two men having previously made a long and painful voyage together in the *Pigot*, and were among the few who survived the mortality with which the crew of that ship was visited'.[4]

This was a reference to *Pigot*'s voyage to Coast and Bay in March 1783. Details of this 'painful voyage' are not known, although the ship returned safely in October 1785.[5] Now, had Meriton and Rogers but known it, another grievous ordeal lay ahead of them.

Fourth Mate Henry Pilcher, was described as of

> 'about twenty-four years of age' and 'a young gentleman highly esteemed'. The son of Edward Pilcher, Esquire, 'one of His Majesty's Justices of the Peace' for the county of Kent, Pilcher had previously served in the Royal Navy as 'a lieutenant on board the *Scipio*—a guardship, commanded by Captain Inglefield'.[6]

William Larkins, Fifth Mate, was the son of Thomas Larkins, Commander of HCS *Warren Hastings*. James Brimer held the title 'supernumerary Fifth Mate', indicating that he was not part of the ship's regular company. A former naval officer, he was *en route* to Madras, where he had relatives and where he hoped to further his career.[7] Sixth Mate was John Daniel.

As regards the officer accommodation, beneath the roundhouse

> … was the great cabin, usually divided into spaces for bachelor army officers and other gentlemen passengers who could not afford the roundhouse. Forward of the great cabin was the steerage, an unpartitioned area normally occupied by cadets, subalterns and clerks travelling on the cheapest fares. On either side of the steerage were cabins for the ship's officers.[8]

Officers and passengers alike were expected to furnish their cabins themselves. The generally accepted minimum requirement was a table, sofa, washstand, cot and bedding. If there was enough room, a couple of chairs and bookshelves were recommended.[9]

In order for a ship to sail speedily and efficiently to destinations thousands of miles away, pinpoint accuracy was required. For example, a regular port of call on the return voyage from the East Indies was the Island of St Helena, situated 800 miles west of the coast of southern Africa.[10] Clearly, the slightest error in navigation could result in failure to locate the correct destination, with the result that the ship was unable to restock with fresh water and food supplies—a potential disastrous eventuality.

In order to determine a ship's location, whilst at sea, it was necessary to ascertain both its latitude and its longitude. The problem of how to determine longitude, however, was a complex one, and it had been solved only as recently as the year 1761, by Yorkshire clockmaker and inventor John Harrison [1693-1776]. Now, with the aid of his marine chronometer, it was possible to calculate longitude—to an accuracy of 18 miles.

A measure of the importance which the Company attached to this matter is indicated by its regulations, which stated that those officers who wished to achieve further promotion, who

> ... have not been already instructed in the method of finding the longitude of a ship at sea, by lunar observations [were advised] immediately [to] perfect themselves under Mr. Lawrence Gwynne at Christ's Hospital, previous to their attending the Committee to be examined for their respective stations; and that they do produce to the Committee the certificate from that gentleman of their being qualified in the method.[11]

*   *   *   *   *

Various items appertaining to navigational skills and seamanship have been retrieved from the wreck, including a brass protractor and a pair of dividers; also a set of shades belonging to a sextant. This instrument, with its graduated arc of 60° and sighting mechanism, was used for measuring the angle that a heavenly body makes with the horizon. The shades were designed to reduce glare when taking visual sightings of the sun. Unfortunately, the smoked glass, which would have varied in intensity for each shade, is missing. (The 'Required Inventory of Equipment etc. necessary for Commanders and Officers' appears in Appendix 4.)

Five midshipmen and four supernumeraries (youths under the care of the captain and officers, but acting as midshipmen)[12] were aboard *Halsewell* when she sailed for Coast and Bay in January 1786. In those times, the majority of midshipmen were the sons of naval officers, or of members of the peerage and landed gentry. Charles Beckford Templer, for example, was the 'brother of James Templer, Esq. His Majesty's Attorney and Master of the Crown-office in the [Court of] King's-bench'. Another, Charles Webber, aged only 13 years,[13] was 'son of the late Admiral Webber and son-in-law to Wm. Smith Esq. of his Majesty's Office of Ordnance'. William Cowley was the 'son of—[First name not known] Cowley, Esq. of Kingston [-upon-Thames] in Surrey'.[14] Thomas Miller was the son of musician and composer Edward Miller, organist of St George's Minster, Doncaster, Yorkshire.

A minority of midshipmen came from commercial or working-class backgrounds. However, 'because of the advantages possessed by the nobility and professional sailors', their chances of promotion to lieutenant were slim.

> Mid-shipmen were expected to work on the ship... learn navigation and seamanship [and how] to rig sails; other duties included keeping watch, relaying messages between decks, supervising gun batteries, commanding small boats, and taking command of a sub-division of the ship's company under one of the lieutenants.[15]

The nickname for a midshipman was 'guinea-pig', which derived from the fact that a), a midshipman in the East India service 'paid an indenture [sum of money paid to the Company under the terms of his contract of employment] of one hundred guineas' and b), 'pig' was the slang term for a naval officer.[16] (The required inventory of equipment etc. necessary for a midshipman appears in Appendix 5.)

Amongst *Halsewell*'s crew, many trades were represented; all necessary for the efficient sailing and maintenance of the ship. These included a surgeon and the surgeon's mates [subordinates]; purser and his assistant; gunner and gunner's mate; boatswain and boatswain's mate; captain's steward; ship's steward; caulker and caulker's mate; cooper (a maker and repairer of casks and barrels).[17] Many had notable connections. For example, 'Mr. Falconer, one of the surgeon's mates, was the son of Magnus Falconer, Esq. one of the master attendants of Chatham [Royal Naval Dock] Yard'. It was his intention to settle at Bencoolen, a city in Sumatra, where the Company had a pepper-trading post and where, at Fort Marlborough, it stationed a garrison. And 'Mr. William Rayner, the purser's assistant, was the son of a gentleman of very respectable abilities in the law...'.[18]

In the trial which was to come, two in particular: the cook Robert Pierce, and the quarter-master James Thompson, would have a crucial role to play, but not in their professional capacities.

The normal complement of ordinary seamen for an East Indiaman was 50;[19] those aboard *Halsewell* being described as 'the best... that could be collected',[20]—a statement that is capable of more than one interpretation! These lower ranks, when not engaged in their duties, occupied below-deck 'steerage' accommodation, which was usually draughty, smelly, and cramped. They slept in hammocks, whereas the higher ranks slept in cots—wooden beds shaped like trays—each with a mattress.

Of particular relevance, in view of the dire situation in which *Halsewell* was shortly to find herself, were the terms and conditions under which her ordinary seamen were employed. Before embarking on a voyage, seamen were paid two months wages in advance, and provision was made for them to be compensated in the event of their injury or death whilst in service with the Company. But in the event of shipwreck (or in nautical terms, if a ship was 'cast away'), or if she was captured by the enemy, what then? This will be discussed shortly.

There were also said to be 'upwards of seventy-three lascars' aboard the ship when she sailed.[21]

*   *   *   *   *

Various artefacts, retrieved from the wreck of *Halsewell* by Wally Hammond, and believed by him to be of no significance, were placed in a bag and put to one side. Said he

> One winter, I decided to take another look at the bag of rubbish and I used my technique to clean these pieces. To my surprise the little bit of metal began to show a design and eventually it showed a Crown, under which was a number 42 and around the edge was a laurel and thistle motif. The button was not a complete disc because about a quarter of it had corroded. However I decided that perhaps it was a soldier's button…

He was correct, for The Black Watch Museum, Perth, Scotland, subsequently confirmed that this was a regimental button from the uniform of a soldier of the 42nd (Royal Highland) Regiment of Foot (known, prior to 1748, as the 43rd Highlanders)—also known as the Black Watch—an infantry regiment of the British Army which was destined for service at Fort St George, Madras. Furthermore, the museum also confirmed that soldiers from the Black Watch had, indeed, been sent to India during this period. Further research in the British Library has resulted in the unearthing of the HEIC's complete list of troops mustered on board the *Halsewell*, on the 24th December 1785 at Gravesend and in the presence of: G. Dominicus of the East India House; George Cooper Surgeon at Gravesend; James Goggan of The East India House together with their county or country of origin, previous occupation, age, and height. 103 persons appear on the list, including Thomas Perryman, sergeant, and Pat Ryan, corporal.[22] However, the muster list does not include the name of the captain and 4 ensigns who would have accompanied them.[23] These findings are in accordance with Henry Meriton's assertion that there was 'a considerable body of soldiers'[24] aboard *Halsewell*.

In regard to *Halsewell*'s passengers, the most expensive cabins for hire, as already indicated, were situated in the roundhouse. Such cabins had portholes—'ports'—which provided their occupants with light and air. Here, female passengers, in particular, enjoyed the advantage of both privacy, and had the protection of the captain, who occupied adjacent premises in the cuddy.[25]

*   *   *   *   *

A finial from a curtain rail, which was recovered from the wreck, probably came from the roundhouse, the portholes of which were curtained—Madras chintz being a favourite material for both curtains and bed-coverings.[26]

It was said by one of *Halsewell*'s officers that the young ladies who sailed aboard her 'were equally distinguished by their beauty and accomplishments'.[27] They included the following. Captain Peirce's two daughters—Eliza (aged 16) and Mary Ann (aged 14)—who 'were going to India to be married to gentlemen of considerable fortune';[28] two of the Captain's nieces—Amy and Mary Paul—the 'daughters of Mr. Paul of Somersetshire';[29] 'Miss [Elizabeth] Blackburne... the daughter of Capt. Blackburne, a commander also in the service of the East India Company, who now resides at Old Malton in Yorkshire'[30] (This was Captain John Blackburn—note spelling, a colleague of Captain Peirce, who, as captain of HCS *Fox*, had sailed in the same fleet as *Halsewell* on the latter ship's first two voyages); the two 'Miss Templers of Bedford Square', who were the sisters of *Halsewell*'s Acting Midshipman Charles B. Templer,[31] whose brother George had married a niece of Captain Peirce. Also, Miss Mary Haggard, 'sister to an officer on the [Madras] establishment'[32]—the HEIC was very much a family affair, and Miss Anne Mansell, 'a native of [Madras], but of European parents', who was 'returning from receiving her education in England'.[33] The only male passenger, as far as is known, was a 'Mr John G. Schultz, Esquire', said by the same officer to be 'amiable in his manners, and of high respect in his character'.[34] Schultz had acquired a very considerable fortune in Asia, from whence he had not been long returned; but some difficulties arising in the collection and remittance of considerable sums which he had left behind him in the East, he found it necessary to make another voyage to Indostan [Hindustan—the Indian subcontinent]....[35]

*   *   *   *   *

Wally Hammond, having retrieved a small, delicate object made of gold, placed it under the scanning electron microscope. Said he, it was

> ... found to have some minute spots of blue enamel on it. I took it to the V and A [Victoria & Albert Museum] in London, and they informed me that it was very likely one face of a four-faced pendant ear-ring. The 5 miniature holes would have contained some type of jewel.

To which of *Halsewell*'s female passengers the earing belonged is not known.

Halsewell's Third Voyage (1786-)

On 16 November 1785

> *Halsewell* was taken up [hired] by the East India Company to make her third voyage to Coast & Bay... and soon fell down to Gravesend, where she completed her lading [i.e. the loading of cargo and provisions].[1]
>
> Whilst the ship lay at Gravesend the Commander [Captain Peirce] was ordered to go aboard her once a week in order to report her condition to the Committee.[2]

Of Captain Peirce, 'it is said he had acquired a competent fortune, and intended that this should be his last voyage'.[3] Now aged 49, he was the Company's oldest serving commander.[4] Meanwhile, his wife Mary had born him a ninth child, 'an infant yet at its mother's breast'.[5]

As for *Halsewell*, once she had completed her third voyage to the East Indies, she was due to be taken out of service. This was according to Company policy, and on account of the excessive wear and tear to her fabric, which such long and arduous journeys entailed. (A century earlier, in 1677, James Vernon, Secretary of State, had paid tribute to the quality of the HEIC's vessels, saying

> one built of the force and strength of those in the East India trade will serve well thirty years in any other trade'. [However] they never use a ship above seven years in that trade, but then turn her off to other trades.[6]

Meanwhile, Thomas Burston senior had died, leaving Peter Esdaile as the ship's sole managing owner.

The inventory of *Halsewell*'s cargo has not survived. However, she was known to be carrying 'general cargo', the nature of which has already been alluded to. Also, 'Silver coin/specie [the two words are synonymous]/ plate'.[7]

Items included under the heading 'General cargo' may, in addition to those already described—namely Spanish reals, dyed cloths, tableware, and glassware—have also included woollens; unmanufactured metals; cutlery; table and kitchen utensils; trinkets, wholly or chiefly of metal; ironmongery of all sorts; locks; bolts; scales and weights; clocks and watches; sheet copper and iron; nails; wire; lead in sheets—cast or rolled; copper pumps; mathematical instruments; fire engines; tinware; fowling shot; bellows; braziery, and all other articles coming under the description of wrought or unwrought metals; canvas, cordage, and marine stores.[8]

The sheet copper was probably destined for Bombay. Here, ships were manufactured both for the HEIC and for the Royal Navy; copper plate being used to clad their hulls. This had the advantage, not only of protecting a vessel and thereby prolonging its life, but also of reducing its frictional resistance through the water, thus enabling it to travel more efficiently.

In addition, *Halsewell*'s cargo may have included zinc; vermilion (a brilliant red pigment made from mercuric sulphide [cinnabar]); velvets and brocades; calico (a type of cotton cloth, typically plain white and unbleached),[9] kersie (a coarse, ribbed cloth with a short nap, woven from short-stapled wool out of which 'kerseys'—working garments—were made); clocks; mechanical toys, and sword-blades.

As for private trade, the *London Recorder & Sunday Gazette* reported, on 15 January 1786, as follows

> We are given to understand that... Captain Peirce had the largest investment on board the *Halsewell* that perhaps had been known for some years, particularly in the fancy line; such as Concave Razors, Olympian Dew [skin care lotion], Metalic Strops, and other useful articles, which are much sought after in India, if they are known to be had from a fashionable house here.[10]

As the date of departure approached, one may imagine the excitement mounting, especially amongst the female passengers for whom there was both the prospect of a great sea voyage; an opportunity to sample the delights of foreign lands; and for Eliza and Mary Ann, daughters of Captain Peirce, as already mentioned, the prospect of marriage. Furthermore, this was an opportunity to be reunited with loved ones. Take Captain Peirce, for example. Calcutta was the home town of his parents, and also, presumably, of his eldest child and namesake, now aged 18, who had sailed to the East Indies with his father on *Halsewell*'s second voyage, where he had remained.[11] In fact, Peirce could look forward to a luxurious sojourn at Madras and

Bengal, his 'dubash'—agent—having procured him a fine mansion, complete with servants.

A senior officer paints the prospect of a delightful picture of life aboard ship, for the privileged few.

> It is hardly possible to conceive a more friendly and happy society, nor one more calculated to join in diverting the tediousness of a long passage, by little plans of rational amusement, and by anticipating the pleasing scenes of novelty, which awaited the accomplishment of their voyage.[12]

To this end, one of the acting midshipmen, Thomas Miller, had been deliberately 'engaged by Captain Peirce to superintend his [the Captain's] 'band of music' and to accompany the young ladies on the piano forte'.[13] Hence the presence on board of the aforementioned viol. Aside from this life of luxury, however, there was a downside, and experienced seafarers, such as Captain Peirce and his senior officers, would have been only too well aware of the dangers attendant on such an enterprise. Not only were there mighty, elemental forces of nature to contended with, but also the ever-present danger of being attacked by the enemy, notably the French, the Dutch, or the Portuguese, or by pirates and privateers. It was a fact that East Indiamen 'burnt, lost or taken [by the enemy]' in the previous twenty years numbered no less than thirty-three.[14]

Company ships in excess of 500 tons 'were compelled to carry a chaplain'.[15] However, this does not appear to have been the case in respect of the 776-ton *Halsewell*, for this or either of her two previous two voyages, during the course of which it was Captain Peirce himself who conducted Sunday services.

Finally, all preparations having been made, it was traditional for the commander and his four most senior officers to present themselves at East India House (the Company's headquarters in London's Leadenhall Street), 'to take their leave of the Court of Directors and receive their sailing instructions'.[16]

The Voyage Begins

Halsewell's first destination, on her third voyage, would be the Portuguese island of Madeira, where she would take on 'water, fruit, vegetables and, most important of all, the local wine, which was very fashionable and popular in India'[1]—if all went according to plan, that was. A first-hand account of the voyage was subsequently provided by Henry Meriton, the ship's Second Mate, who survived, despite his life, quite literally, hanging by a thread.

HCS *Ganges*, 758 tons, had sailed with *Halsewell* on her first voyage, when it was reported that she was 'missing from the fleet' and had not been seen 'since we left Madeira'. It was not until the following month at Goree, Senegal, that she was reunited with the fleet. It was hoped that no such misfortune would befall either ship on this forthcoming voyage when *Ganges* would, once again, be *Halsewell*'s companion, having rendezvoused with her at Portsmouth.

Having taken 'the ladies and other passengers on board at the Hope', *Halsewell* 'sailed through The Downs'[2]—a seaway or 'roadstead' off Deal on the east coast of Kent—on Sunday 1 January 1786. On the morning of Monday 2 January, when she was 'a-breast of Dunnose' (Dunnose Point near Ventnor on the southern coast of the Isle of Wight) said Meriton, 'it felt calm'.[3] However

> ... at three in the afternoon, a breeze sprung up from the South, when they ran in shore to land the pilot, but very thick weather coming on in the evening, and the wind baffling [i.e. perplexing], at nine in the evening they were obliged to anchor in eighteen fathom [one fathom = 6 feet] [of] water....

In other words, adverse weather prevented the pilot from disembarking.

[They] furled [reefed—i.e. rolled up or gathered up] their top-sails, but could not furl their courses [the lowest sails on the mast], the snow falling thick, and freezing as it fell.[4]

On Tuesday 3 January

... at four in the morning, a strong gale came on from East-North East, and the ship driving [being blown by the wind with great force], they were obliged to cut their cables and run off [i.e. further out] to sea. At noon, they spoke with a brig bound to Dublin, and having put their pilot on board her, bore down channel immediately. At eight in the evening, the wind freshening and coming to [i.e. from] the Southward, they reefed such sails as were judged necessary.

At ten at night it blew a violent gale of wind at [i.e. from the] South, and they were obliged to carry a press of sail [the greatest amount of sail that a ship can carry safely under prevailing conditions] to keep the ship off shore, in doing which the hawse plugs [canvas bags filled with oakum and used to plug the hawse-holes—reinforced apertures in the ship's bows through which the anchor cables passed—in order to keep out sea water], which according to a new improvement were put inside, were washed in, and the hawse bags washed away, in consequence of which they shipped a large quantity of water on the gun deck.

The ship's bilge well (i.e. the lowest internal portion of the hull) was now sounded,[5] and water was discovered in her bilges to a depth of 5 feet.[6] The leak having been discovered, continued Meriton, 'all the pumps were set to work'.[7] In addition, in order to prevent *Halsewell* from heeling, and thereby taking in even more water

... they clued [clewed] the main top-sail up [i.e. took in the sail by hoisting its lower corners to the yard], hauled up the main-sail, and immediately endeavoured to furl both, but could not effect it....[8]

The situation was becoming increasingly desperate. On Wednesday 4 January

... at two in the morning, they endeavoured to wear the ship [i.e. 'gybe'— whereby a vessel which is sailing downwind manoeuvres in such a way that the wind now comes from its opposite side], but without success, and judging it necessary to cut away the miz[z]en mast [the mast aft of a ship's mainmast] it was immediately done, and a second attempt made to wear the ship, which succeeded no better than the former...

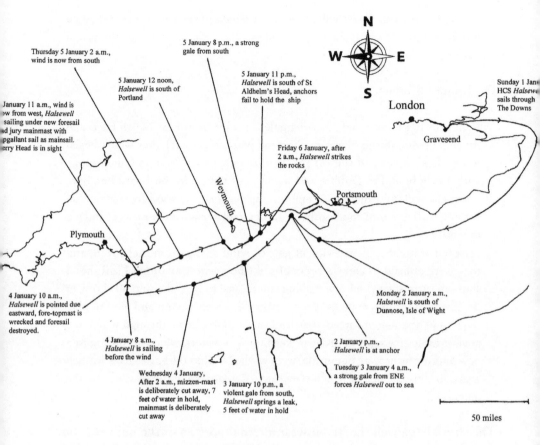

Thursday 5 January 2 a.m.,
wind is now from south

5 January 8 p.m., a strong
gale from south

5 January 12 noon,
Halsewell is south of
Portland

5 January 11 p.m.,
Halsewell is south of St
Aldhelm's Head, anchors
fail to hold the ship

N
W   E
S

London

Gravesend

Sunday 1 Janu
HCS *Halsewe
sails through
The Downs

January 11 a.m., wind is
ow from west, *Halsewell*
sailing under new foresail
d jury mainmast with
pgallant sail as mainsail.
erry Head is in sight

Friday 6 January, after
2 a.m., *Halsewell* strikes
the rocks

Weymouth

Portsmouth

Plymouth

4 January 10 a.m.,
Halsewell is pointed due
eastward, fore-topmast is
wrecked and foresail
destroyed.

Monday 2 January a.m.,
Halsewell is south of
Dunnose, Isle of Wight

4 January 8 a.m.,
Halsewell is sailing
before the wind

2 January p.m.,
Halsewell is at anchor

Tuesday 3 January 4 a.m.,
a strong gale from ENE
forces *Halsewell* out to sea

Wednesday 4 January,
After 2 a.m., mizzen-mast
is deliberately cut away, 7
feet of water in hold,
mainmast is deliberately
cut away

3 January 10 p.m., a
violent gale from south,
Halsewell springs a leak,
5 feet of water in hold

50 miles

English Channel, January 1786: the final voyage of HCS *Halsewell*.

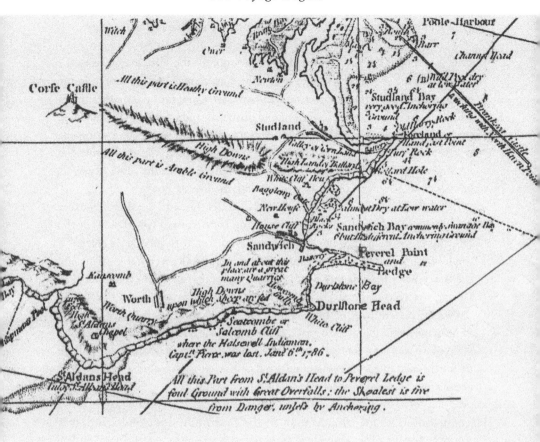

Chart of South Coast of Dorsetshire, 1721, from Joseph Avery.

With 7 feet of water in her hold, and the pumps unable to keep pace

> ... it was thought expedient, for the preservation of the ship, to cut away the
> main mast, the ship appearing to be in immediate danger of foundering; in the
> fall of the mast, Jonathan Moreton, cockswain [*sic*], and four men, either fell or
> were drawn by the wreck over-board and drowned, and by eight in the morning
> the wreck was cleared, and the ship got before the wind in which position she
> was kept about two hours, in which time the pumps cleared the ship of two feet
> of water in the hold [i.e. the level fell to 5 feet]: At this time the ship's head [i.e.
> her bows] was brought to the East-ward with the fore-sail only.
>
> At ten in the morning the wind abated considerably, and the ship labouring
> extremely, rolled the fore top-mast over on the larboard [port] side, in the
> fall the wreck went through the fore-sail, and tore it to pieces. At eleven in
> the forenoon, the wind came to the Westward, and the weather clearing up,
> the Berry-head [east-facing headland at the southern extremity of Tor Bay,
> Devonshire] was distinguishable bearing North and by East, [i.e. 11° 25' East
> of North] distant four or five leagues [i.e. 12–15 nautical miles]; they now
> immediately bent [secured to yard] another fore-sail, erected a jury [makeshift]
> main-mast, and set a top-gallant-sail for a main-sail, under which sail they bore
> up for [headed towards] Portsmouth, and employed the remainder of the day in
> getting up a jury mizen-mast.[9]

Here, it should be mentioned that, in the face of an opposing wind, it was
impossible for a sailing ship such as *Halsewell* to achieve a 'point of sail' (i.e.
the angle between the direction in which the ship is sailing and that from
which the wind is blowing) of less than about 85° to 80°.[10] In other words,
Halsewell was able to sail at little more than 90° to the wind. In her stricken
state, therefore, the possibility of her making any headway whatever against
the prevailing westerly wind, was virtually non-existent. On Thursday 5
January

> ... at two in the morning, the wind came to [i.e. from] the Southward, blew
> fresh, and the weather was very thick; at noon Portland was seen bearing North
> and by East, distant two or three leagues.

The so-called 'Isle of Portland' which is, in fact, a peninsula, stretches five
miles out to sea south of the Dorsetshire town of Weymouth. At the time
in question, two lighthouses were situated here at Portland Bill—a narrow
promontory near to the southern tip of the island.

> At eight at night it blew a strong gale at South, and at this time the Portland
> lights were seen bearing North-West [i.e. 45° West of North] distant four or

five leagues, when they wore the ship, and got her head to the Westward...[11] but finding they lost ground on that tack, they wore her again, and kept stretching [presumably progressing slowly] on to the Eastward, in hopes to have weathered [safely negotiated] Peverel-Point.[12]

Peveril Point (note spelling) is a promontory at the southern extremity of Swanage Bay on the east-facing coast of Dorsetshire's Isle of Purbeck (which is, in fact, a peninsula). Had Captain Peirce succeeded in weathering the point, it would have been possible for him to anchor in Studland Bay, which faces east and is therefore protected from the prevailing westerly winds. Alas, the captain's efforts were in vain.

At eleven at night it cleared, and they saw St. Alban's-head* a mile and [a] half to the leeward of them [i.e. on the opposite side of the ship from which the wind was blowing], upon which they took in sail immediately, and let go the small bower anchor, which brought up the ship at a whole cable [i.e. by letting out the entire length of the anchor's cable] and she rode [was anchored to the sea bed] for about an hour, but then drove [was impelled by wind and/or tide]; they now let go the sheet anchor [reserve anchor for use in emergencies] and wore away a whole cable [let out its entire length], and the ship rode for about two hours longer, when she drove again [the anchor having failed to hold her].[13]

*The correct name of the aforementioned headland is St Aldhelm's Head, which was described, ominously, by surgeon, traveller and author Sir Frederick Treves (1853-1923), as follows

Standing boldly out into the sea, it faces the Channel with a bald cliff 350 feet in height [an understatement by Treves—see below]. At its foot is a most inhospitable shore of rocks. On the summit of St. Alban's Head is a tiny Norman chapel, square and low, built of walls so thick that there is little space within.

Built in about 1080, the chapel is dedicated to Saint Aldhelm (*c*. AD 640–AD 709), Anglo-Saxon scholar and prelate who became first Bishop of Sherbourne, Dorsetshire in AD 705. Here, in winter, said Treves, there could often be heard 'the shrieking of the wind and the lashing of the hail...'.[14]

Having been sent for by Captain Peirce, said Meriton, he was

asked his opinion as to the probability of saving their lives, to which he replied with equal calmness and candour, that he apprehended [that] there was very little hope, as they were then driving fast on the shore, and might expect every moment to strike; the [ship's] boats were then mentioned, but it was agreed that at the time they could be of no use, yet in case an opportunity should present itself of making them serviceable, it was proposed that the officers should be confidentially requested to reserve the long-boat for the ladies and themselves, and this precaution was immediately taken.[15]

On Friday 6 January at 'about two in the morning' with 'the ship still driving, and approaching very fast to the shore', Captain Peirce again expressed his

... extreme anxiety for the preservation of his beloved daughters, and earnestly asking the officer if he could devise any means of saving them.

To this, Meriton replied

... with great concern that he feared it would be impossible, but that their only chance would be to wait for the morning, [whereupon] the Captain lifted up his hands in silent and distressful ejaculation.

At this dreadful moment the ship struck with such violence as to dash the heads of those who were standing in the cuddy, against the deck above them, and the fatal blow was accompanied by a shriek of horror, which burst at one instant from every quarter of the ship.[16]

Shipwreck

Sir Frederick Treves described, in detail, that section of the southern coastline of Dorsetshire's 'Isle of Purbeck' that lies between the coastal town of Swanage (centre of the stone trade) to the east, and the port of Weymouth (25 miles distant) to the west, with its

> … cliffs of jagged rocks, sheer as a bastion wall, as well as green lawns which creep lazily to the water's edge. There are wide, open bays, and fissured sea-echoing chines [narrow ravines]. There are round coves, inlets reached through arched rocks, level sands, and moaning caves. There are beaches of shingle, of pebbles, of colossal boulders, and of the clay of crumbling banks; precipices of every colour, from the white of chalk to the black of the shale; and walls of stone streaked with tints of yellow, buff, or red.

More specifically, Treves described that section which lay immediately to the west of Swanage, where

> … the coast is drab and savage, the cliffs erect or scooped out in places by quarries. There is no beach. The rock rampart, cracked by sinister rents, rises from the sea above evil-looking ledges and follows the sea halls [presumably caverns, cut out of the rock by the action of the sea].[1]

Therefore, of all the places on the coast for *Halsewell* to have foundered, this was amongst the worst. Meriton himself describes this 'deplorable scene'.

> The ship struck on the rocks at or near Seacombe, on the Island of Purbeck, between Peverel-Point, and St. Alban's Head, at a part of the shore where the cliff is of vast height, and rises almost perpendicular from its base.

But at this particular spot the cliff is excavated at the foot, and presents a cavern of ten or twelve yards in depth, and of breadth equal to the length of a large ship, the sides of the cavern so nearly upright as to be extremely difficult of access, the roof formed of the stupendous cliff, and the bottom of it strewed with sharp and uneven rocks, which seem to have been rent from above by some convulsion of nature. It was at the mouth of this cavern that the unfortunate wreck lay stretched almost from side to side of it, and offering her broadside to the horrible chasm.[2]

For Captain Peirce, and doubtless for his more experienced officers and crew (who had faced the hazards of foreign climes during the course of numerous voyages half way around the world), the irony of being shipwrecked on their very own shores would not have been lost on them. But what was perhaps a greater irony, was that had the crew not been deliberately neglectful of their duty, the whole tragedy might have been averted. So much is evident from Meriton's account.

The seamen, many of whom had been remarkably inattentive and remiss in their duty during [the] great part of the storm, and had actually skulked in their hammocks, and left the exertions of the pump, and the other labours attending their situation, to the officers of the ship, and the soldiers; (who had been uncommonly active and assiduous during the whole tremendous conflict)...

What could have possessed the seamen to behave with such apparent disregard for their own safety, let alone that of anybody else? The explanation appeared a few days later in the *London Recorder & Sunday Gazette*, where it was stated that the loss of *Halsewell*

... is attributed, in a great measure to the want of subordination in the crew, as while there was a probability of saving it [the ship], the seamen absolutely refused to obey the officers, and on being threatened with chastisements, exultingly answered in the following laconic indolent manner—'You be d—n'd: If you dare, d—n my eyes, but I'll Loughborough you.'—alluding, as is supposed, to a late verdict in the Court of Common Pleas.[3]

This was a reference to lawyer Lord Loughborough (Alexander Wedderburn, 1st Earl of Rosslyn, 1733-1805) who had presided over the aforementioned court, where he

... afforded relief to a body of ... seafaring men who, in the course of long voyages to the East Indies, America, and the coast of Africa, were not unfrequently exposed to cruelty and injustice on the part of their officers, while they were not always able to contend, on their return, with the real or supposed offenders by means of an expensive suit at law. Several noted cases of this kind were tried before his lordship; and the damages awarded tended not a little to check brutal usage on the part of commanders and inferior officers.[4]

In other words, if their officers punished the crewman unduly harshly and the latter complained, it was in the knowledge that the law would protect them. But surely here, the context was quite different, in that it was not Captain Peirce and his officers who posed a threat, but the elemental forces of nature which threatened to overwhelm them. Also, prior to the Merchant Shipping Act of 1854,

> … the principle then recognised by the courts [was] that 'freight is the mother of [i.e. source of] wages'. Under that phrase a seaman's right to wages depended on the ship's earning of freight, so that, if she were lost of taken [i.e. captured] before the end of the voyage, or at any rate before her arrival at her destination for delivery of the cargo, the mariners lost all claim to wages.

(However, the captain of such a ship was exempt from this rule.)[5] Therefore, quite apart from the necessity of self-preservation, surely this was another compelling reason for *Halsewell*'s seamen to assist in trying to save the ship. Finally, said Meriton, 'rouzed [*sic*] by the destructive blow'—i.e. the ship striking the rocks—'to a sense of their danger', the seamen

> … now poured upon the deck…, and in frantic exclamations demanded of heaven and their fellow-sufferers, that succour, which their timely efforts might possibly have succeeded in procuring; but it was now too late, the ship continued to beat on the rocks, and soon bulged [i.e. the hull bulged outwards due to the pressure of the incoming water], and fell with her broad side towards the shore: When the ship struck, a number of the men climbed up the ensign staff [wooden pole at the stern of the vessel from which the ensign flag is flown], under an apprehension of her going to pieces immediately.[6]

Whereupon, Meriton

> … offered to these unhappy beings the best advice which could possibly be given to them; he recommended their coming all to that side of the ship which lay lowest on the rocks, and singly to take the opportunities which might then offer of escaping to the shore. And having thus provided to the utmost of his power, for the safety of the desponding crew, he returned to the roundhouse, where by this time all the passengers, and most of the officers were assembled.…[7]

At the time the ship struck, said Meriton, 'it was too dark to discover the extent of their danger, and the extreme horror of their situation...'. Nevertheless, he

> ... conceived a hope that she [*Halsewell*] might keep together till day-light, and endeavoured to chear [cheer] his drooping friends, and in particular the unhappy ladies, with this comfortable expectation....[8]
>
> In addition to the company already in the roundhouse, they had admitted three black women and two soldiers' wives, who with the husband of one of them had been permitted to come in, though the seamen who had tumultuously demanded entrance, to get the lights [presumably access to the lanterns], had been opposed, and kept out by Mr. Rogers, the Third Mate, and Mr. Brimer, the Fifth, so that the numbers there were now increased to near fifty; Captain Peirce sitting on a chair, cot, or some other moveable [object], with a daughter on each side of him, each of whom he alternately pressed to his affectionate bosom; the rest of the melancholy assembly were seated on the deck, which was strewed with musical instruments, and the wreck of furniture, trunks, boxes and packages.

(The presence of black people aboard *Halsewell* may possibly be accounted for as follows)

> English gentlemen who had been for some years under the Company in India, either in a civil or military capacity, were often wont to bring black servants home with them, and after these servants had been some time in England they were discharged. The result was that, under the terms of their obligation, the Company were put to great expense in sending them back to their native country.)[9]

Continuing his account of the shipwreck, Meriton

> ... having previously cut several wax candles into pieces, and stuck them up in various parts of the roundhouse, and lighted up all the glass lanthorns [lanterns] he could find, took his seat, intending to wait the happy dawn, that might present to him the means of effecting his own escape, and afford him an opportunity of giving assistance to the partners of his danger [i.e., fellow sufferers], but observing the poor ladies appeared parched and exhausted, he fetched a basket of oranges from some part of the roundhouse, and prevailed on some of them to refresh themselves by sucking a little of the juice. At this time they were all tolerably composed, except Miss Mansel, who was in hysteric fits on the floor deck of the roundhouse.

'The Affecting situation of Capt. Pierce and the LADIES his DAUGHTERS, NEICES &c in the Round House of the *Halsewell*, East India Man, just before the sinking of the Wreck.' Engraved for the *New Lady's Magazine*, published by Alexander Hogg at the King's Arms, No. 16 Paternoster Row, 1 March 1786.

But on his return to the company, he perceived considerable alteration in the appearance of the ship, the sides were visibly giving way, the deck seemed to be lifting, and he discovered other strong symptoms that she could not hold together much longer, he therefore attempted to go forward to look out, but immediately saw that the ship was separated in the middle, and that the fore part had changed its position, and lay rather farther out towards the sea; and in this emergency, when the next moment might be charged with his fate, he determined to seize the present, and to follow the example of the crew, and the soldiers, who were now quitting the ship in numbers, and making their way to ashore, of which they knew not yet the horrors.

Among other measures adopted to favour these attempts, the ensign-staff had been unshipped, and attempted to be lain from the ship's side to some of the rocks, but without success, for it snapped to pieces before it reached them, however by the light of a lanthorn, which a seaman, of the name of Burmaster [whose name does not appear in Meriton's list of survivors], handed through the sky-light of the roundhouse to the deck, Mr. Meriton discovered a spar, which appeared to be laid from the ship side to the rocks, and on this spar he determined to attempt his escape.

He accordingly laid himself down on it, and thrust himself forward, but he soon found that the spar had no communication with the rock, he reached the end of it, and then slipped off, receiving a very violent bruise in his fall, and before he could recover his legs, he was washed off by the surge, in which he supported himself by swimming, till the returning wave dashed him against the back part of the cavern, where he laid hold of a small projecting piece of the rock, but was so benumbed, that he was on the point of quitting it, when a seaman who had already gained a footing, extended his hand, and assisted him till he could secure himself on a little of the rock, from which he clambered [onto a] shelf still higher, till he was out of the reach of the surf.

Meriton therefore owed his life to these two seamen.

Less than a mile inland from the stricken *Halsewell* lies the village of Worth Matravers (Worth), whose Parish Register for 1786 pays tribute to First Mate Thomas Burston.

The Chief Mate said, in the fatal moment when the Second Mate [Meriton] was quitting the ship, that he would die with his uncle, the captain, and his cousins, the Miss Peirces; for, were he to leave such dear relatives behind him, he could only expect the worst of deaths, to be discarded for ever from the service [i.e. that of the East India Company]![10]

*   *   *   *   *

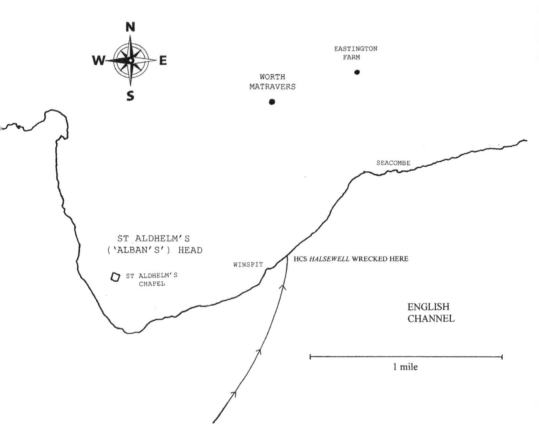

The site of the shipwreck.

Two centuries later, as already mentioned, a button from the uniform of Thomas Burston bearing the monogram 'TB' was recovered from the wreck. Also recovered was his personal stamp; it too bore the initials 'TB', but in mirror image, and on the reverse, a foul anchor motif (anchor entwined with a cable wound around its flukes). Less than ¼ inch in thickness it was made of green coloured glass. This, Burston would have used to make his mark on the wax with which he sealed his personal correspondence and important documents.

*   *   *   *   *

Continued Meriton

Mr. Rogers, the third mate remained with the Captain, and the unfortunate ladies, and their companions, near twenty minutes after Mr. Meriton had quitted the ship: Soon after the latter left the roundhouse, the Captain asked what was become of him, and Mr. Rogers replied that he was gone on the deck, to see what could be done.—After this a heavy sea breaking over the ship, the ladies exclaimed, 'Oh poor Meriton, he is drowned, had he stayed with us he would have been safe,' and they all, and particularly Miss Mary Peirce, expressed great concern at the apprehension of his loss.

At this time the sea was breaking in at the fore part of the ship, and reached as far as the main-mast, and Captain Peirce gave Mr. Rogers a nod, and they took a lamp, and went together into the stern galley [enclosed platform at the stern of the ship], and after viewing the rocks for some time, Captain Peirce asked Mr. Rogers, if he thought there was any possibility of saving the girls, to which he replied, he feared there was not, for they could only discover the black face of the perpendicular rock, and not the cavern which afforded shelter to those who escaped; they then returned to the roundhouse, and Mr. Rogers hung up the lamp, and Captain Peirce, with his great coat on, sat down between his two daughters, and struggled to suppress the parental tear which then burst into his eye.

The sea continuing to break in very fast, Mr. McManus, a midshipman, and Mr. Schu[l]tz, a passenger, asked Mr. Rogers what they could do to escape, who replied 'follow me,' and they then all went into the stern gallery and from thence by the weather upper quarter gallery [balconies on the port and starboard sides of the sterncastle] upon the poop [deck], and whilst they were there a very heavy sea fell on board, and the roundhouse gave way, and he heard the ladies shriek at intervals, as if the water had reached them, the noise of the sea at other times drowning their voices.

Mr. Brimer [Fifth Mate] had followed Mr. Rogers to the poop, where they remained together about five minutes, when on the coming on of the last mentioned sea, they jointly seized a hen-coop, and the same wave which he apprehended proved fatal to some of those who remained below, happily carried him and his companion to the rock, on which they were dashed with such violence as to be miserably bruised and hurt.

On this rock were twenty-seven men, but it was low water, and as they were convinced that upon the flowing of the tide, they must all be washed off, many of them attempted to get to the back or sides of the Cavern, out of the reach of the returning sea, [but] in this attempt scarce more then six, besides himself [Rogers], and Mr. Brimer succeeded, of the remainder some shared the fate which they had apprehended, and the others perished in their efforts to get into the Cavern.

Mr. Rogers and Mr. Brimer both however reached the cavern, and scrambled up the rock, on narrow shelves of which they fixed themselves, Mr. Rogers got so near to his friend Mr. Meriton as to exchange congratulations with him, but he was prevented from joining him by at least twenty men who were between them, neither of whom could move without immediate peril of his life. At the time Mr. Rogers reached the station of possible safety, his strength was so nearly exhausted, that had the struggle continued a few minutes longer he must have been inevitably lost.

They now found that a very considerable number of the crew, seamen, soldiers, and some petty officers were in the same situation with themselves, tho' many who had reached the rocks below, had perished, in attempting to ascend; what that situation was they were still to learn; at present they had escaped immediate death, but they were yet to encounter cold, nakedness, wind, rain, and the perpetual beating of the spray of the sea, for a difficult, precarious, and doubtful chance of escape.

They could yet discern some part of the ship, and solaced themselves, in their dreary stations, with the hope of its remaining entire till daybreak, for, in the midst of their own misfortunes, the sufferings of the females affected them with the most acute anguish, and every sea that broke, brought with it terror, for the fate of those amiable and helpless beings.

The sound of *Halsewell*, their erstwhile home, being pummelled to pieces against the rocks, her timbers creaking, groaning, and splitting under the strain, must have been truly terrifying.

But, alas! their apprehensions were too soon realised. In a very few minutes after Mr. Rogers had gained the rock, an universal shriek, which still vibrates in their ears, and in which, the voice of female distress was lamentably distinguishable, announced the dreadful Catastrophe; in a few moments all was hushed, except the warring winds, and beating waves; the wreck was buried in the remorseless deep, and not an atom of her was ever after discoverable.[10]

... many of those who had gained the precarious stations which we have described, worn out with fatigue, weakened by bruises, battered by the tempest, and benumbed with the cold, quitted their holdfasts, and tumbling headlong either on the rocks below, or in the surf, perished beneath the feet of their wretched associates, and by their dying groans, and gulping exclamations for pity, awakened terrific apprehensions in the survivors, of their own approaching fate.

At length, after the bitterest three hours which misery ever lengthened into ages, the day broke on them, but instead of bringing with it the relief with which they had flattered themselves, served to discover all the horrors of their situation... they were completely ingulfed [*sic*] in the cavern, and over-hung by the cliff, nor did any part of the wreck remain to point out their probable place of refuge; below, no [potential rescue] boat could live [survive in such conditions] to search them out, and had it been possible to have acquainted those who would wish to assist them, with their exact situation, no ropes could be conveyed into the cavity, to facilitate their escape.

In fact, said Meriton, 'Guns of distress' had been fired by *Halsewell* 'for many hours before the ship struck', but because of 'the violence of the storm were unheard' by any potential rescuer on shore.[11]

A Glimmer of Hope

For those who had survived that terrible night, said Meriton

> The only prospect which offered, was to creep along the side of the cavern, to its outward extremity, and on a ledge scarcely as broad as a man's hand, to turn the corner, and endeavour to clamber up the almost perpendicular precipice, whose summit was near two hundred feet from the base.[1]

(The cliffs at this point are, in fact, approximately 100 feet above sea level.) However, in their 'desperate effort' to climb the sheer cliff face, said he, some succeeded

> ... whilst others, trembling with terror, and their strength exhausted by mental and bodily fatigue, lost their precarious footing, and perished in the attempt. The first men who gained the summit of the cliff, were the Cook [Robert Pierce], and James Thompson, a quarter-master, by their own exertions they made their way to the land, and the moment they reached it, hastened to the nearest house, and made known the situation of their fellow-sufferers.[2]

Even for the seamen, who were used to shinning up the ship's rigging, this would have been a noteworthy feat, but for men such as these, it was a truly remarkable one.

The aforementioned 'house' was 'Eastington', situated about a mile to the east of Worth Matravers and currently the abode of Thomas Garland, 'steward or agent to the proprietors of the Purbeck Quarries'.[3]

The village of Worth, said Sir Frederick Treves, was

... built wholly of stone, but boasting a few trees. The landscape around it is reduced to two elements only—bare grass and the sea.[4]

As for the source of the stone, journalist, writer, and educator Arthur H. Mee, declared that 'the whole country round is honey-combed with quarries...'.[5] And as it transpired, it was to the quarrymen of Worth and district that the vast majority of those who survived the disaster owed their lives. (Here, it is pointed out that although there are cliff quarries all along this coast, accessed from a ledge about 40 feet below the cliff top, there was evidently no such quarry immediately above the cavern where *Halsewell* came to grief.)

Worth's church, which dates from the 12th century, is dedicated to Nicholas, 4th century Bishop of Myra in Asia Minor (modern-day Turkey). Nicholas is the patron saint of fishermen, scholars, children, and sailors— but, alas, on this occasion there was to be no saintly intervention on behalf of the stricken East Indiaman *Halsewell*.

It is the church's vicar, the Reverend Morgan Jones who now takes up the story.

I was sitting at breakfast with Mr. Garland on Friday the 6th of January, when news was brought, that a large ship was on shore. The disposition of the country to plunder is well known; we therefore immediately mounted our horses, to afford what protection we could to the unfortunate. But the fury of the wind, the violence of the rain, thick fog and deep snow, frustrated our endeavours after three hours riding round the coast. We then met with three poor wretches who had escaped from the general ruin, over the cliffs, they were in a most distressed state at Worth [N.B. This account is somewhat at variance with that of Meriton]. We removed them to a better house, and left them in good beds, and well provided, and then proceeded with a guide to the fatal spot. But such a horrid, tremendous scene never did my eyes behold, and God of His mercy grant that they may never again. The sea ran mountains high, and lashed the rocks with all the appearance of insolence and anger. The ship, which struck at two in the morning, was so entirely beat to pieces, that nothing but the whole ocean covered with her fragments could have persuaded me that she had ever been drifted together [i.e. have ever have been a whole]. In one place lay her rigging, etc., wound up like the garbage of an animal and rolling to and fro in sullen submission to the imperious waves. In the different recesses of the rocks, a confused heap of boards, broken masts, chests, trunks, and dead bodies, were huddled together, and a face of the water as far as the eye could extend was disfigured with floating carcasses, tables, chairs, casks, and part of every other article in the vessel.[6]

Mr Garland, said Meriton

> ... immediately got together the workmen under his direction, and with the most zealous and animated humanity, exerted every effort for the preservation of the surviving crew of this unfortunate ship; ropes were procured with all possible despatch, and every precaution taken that assistance should be speedily and effectually given...

The quarrymen were now, on this bitterly cold winter's morning, to participate in one of the most dramatic rescues ever to have been effected on the coast of Britain. Meanwhile, Meriton, writing about himself, as usual, in the third person, describes how he himself 'made the attempt' to scale the cliff

> ... and almost reached the edge of the precipice; a soldier who preceded him, had his feet on a small projecting rock or stone, and on the same stone Mr. Meriton had fastened his hands to help his progress; at this critical moment the Quarry-men arrived, and seeing a man so nearly within their reach, they dropped a rope to him, of which he immediately laid hold, and in a vigorous effort to avail himself of this advantage, he loosened the stone on which he stood, which giving way, Mr. Meriton must have been precipitated to the bottom, but that a rope was providentially lowered to him at the instant, which he seized as he was in the act of falling, and was safely drawn to the summit.[7]

The Reverend Morgan Jones described how others survived

> ... by being carried on pieces of the wreck to parts more easily gained. The Fourth Mate [Henry Pilcher] and about 40 of the men followed the Second [Meriton] as far as they dared, and then waited in painful suspense, till they were drawn up by a rope let down by the quarriers. Another party of 30, worse situated, or unable to gain a higher part, were seen to be washed from the rock on which they stood by one furious wave, at the return of the morning tide. The arrival of Mr. Garland and myself proved fortunate for about 20 more unhappy wretches, who were discovered under the shelter of a large chasm or cavern in the rock, about 30 feet from the bottom [i.e. just as Meriton had explained]. The quarriers were worn with fatigue, cold, wet and hunger; and were more eager to get their share of two casks of spirit which had just been sent them, than to attend to the cries of the sufferers below; nor was there any one person of sufficient authority to encourage or direct them.

The Reverend Morgan Jones and Mr Garland now took charge of the situation. Said the former

Our presence occasioned a proper application of the liquor, prevented all intoxication, and saved many of them [the quarrymen] from tumbling down the precipice; and our promises of reward cheered them to proceed with vigour, till we had drawn up every one that remained alive.

The method of saving the last was singular, and does honour to the humanity and intrepidity of the quarriers. The distance from the top of rock to the cranny was about 60 feet, with a projection of the former of about eight feet, ten of these sixty feet formed a declivity to the edge, and the remaining fifty feet were quite perpendicular.

On the very brink of the precipice, stood two daring fellows, a rope being tied round their bodies, and fastened above to a strong iron bar, fixed in the ground; behind them, in like manner, two more. A large cable also, properly secured, passed between them, by which they might hold and support themselves from falling; they then lay down a rope, with a noose ready fixed, below the cavern; and the wind blowing hard, forced it under the projecting rock sufficiently for the men to reach it. Whoever caught it put the noose round his waist; and after escaping from one element; committed himself in full swing, to another, in which he dangled till he was drawn [up] with great care and caution. We brought up 18 in this manner; three died before we could assist them; they were all senseless when we received them, and certainly bruised; but we had brought cherry-brandy and gingerbread with us, and by supplying them with small quantities of ale, we soon recovered them, and sent them to a farm-house, where they were supplied with every possible assistance. The surviving officers, seamen and soldiers, being now assembled at the house of their benevolent friend, Mr. Garland they were mustered and found to amount to 74, out of more than 240....

Is 240 a realistic figure for the number of persons aboard *Halsewell* when she sailed? According to Meriton, the number of 'officers' (i.e. those other than ordinary seamen, lascars, or passengers) was 39. There were also 50 seamen (an approximate estimate); 108 soldiers, including their captain, and 4 ensigns; 15 women (according to the Reverend Morgan Jones—which included three black women and two soldiers' wives referred to by Meriton);[8] one male passenger, and (upwards of) 73 lascars. This gives an overall total of 286. The figure of 240, given by the Reverend Jones, is therefore an underestimate. However, according to Meriton, as

all books and papers went to the bottom with *Halsewell*, it has been impossible to obtain an exact list of all the seamen, soldiers,[9] and passengers, and servants, who were on board her at the time she sailed, nor is the list of the officers perfectly complete, some of the more subordinate being usually entered on the ship's books, at the time they actually come on board.[10]

Said a grateful Meriton

> … we are happy in this opportunity of bearing testimony, under the authority of the principal surviving officers, to the kind, benevolent, and spirited behaviour of this Gentleman [Thomas Garland], whose conduct in the melancholy occasion, entitles him to universal respect and regard, as well as to the particular gratitude of those who were the immediate objects of his philanthropy.[11]

And in addition to the assistance received from Mr Garland and the quarrymen, said Meriton

> … it is but justice in this place to say, that the survivors received the friendly and humane assistance of Mr. Jones and Mr. Hawker, gentlemen resident near the spot.[12]

This 'Mr. Hawker' was George Ryves Hawker, Rector of Wareham's Churches of Holy Trinity with St Mary and St Martin (since 1773), who was probably visiting his colleague, the Reverend Morgan Jones, at the time.[13]

Last, but not least, William Trenton, a soldier whose name appeared on the list of survivors, had

> … remained on his perilous stand till the morning of Saturday the 7th of January, exposed to the united horrors of the extremest personal danger, and the most acute disquietude of mind; nor is it easy to conceive how his strength and spirits could have supported him for such a number of hours, under distress so poignant and complicated.[14]

In other words, Trenton had been exposed to the elements for in excess of 30 hours.

In Worth Matravers' parish register, the Reverend Morgan Jones stated of *Halsewell*, 'Never did happen so complete a wreck, the Ship long before day-break was shattered all to Pieces…'.[15] As for the financial loss to the HEIC, *The Times* newspaper reported that this did not exceed '6,000 l' (i.e. £6,000).[16] (This would have been principally represented by the value of the cargo, for its owner Peter Esdaile, would be obliged to bear the capital loss of the vessel herself.)

Aftermath: *Halsewell*'s Grim Legacy

On Saturday 7 January 1786, the day after the shipwreck, said Meriton, he and his comrade John Rogers, who was also numbered amongst the survivors

> … having been liberally assisted by Mr. Garland with the means of making the journey, set off for London, to carry the melancholy tidings to the Directors of the India-House; and having humanely taken the precaution to acquaint the magistrates of the towns through which they passed, that a number of shipwrecked men would be soon on the road to the metropolis, they arrived at the India-House on Sunday the 8th instant at noon.…[1]

The following day, Monday 9 January, the Reverend Hawker wrote from Wareham to Thomas Southcomb Esquire of Gate Street Lincolns Inn Fields, to inform him that the remaining survivors from *Halsewell*

> … have just left this Town, where all their present wants have been supplied by the Inhabitants with a liberality that does them honor, a few sick are left behind, and they shall be taken care of.[2]

Meriton singled out one particular individual for praise, saying

> It would be unjust to suppress the circumstance, which reflects great honour on the benevolence of the master of the Crown Inn, at Blandford, Dorsetshire. When the distressed seamen arrived in that town, he sent for them all to his house, and having given them the refreshment of a comfortable dinner, he presented each man with a crown to help him on his journey.[3]

Meanwhile, at India House, said Meriton

> ... the sad tale was no sooner told, than the Directors, with their usual munificence, ordered handsome gratifications to the Quarry-men and others, who assisted in saving the survivors, and provided some immediate support for those who out-lived this lamentable event. To Mr. Garland the Directors have also made such acknowledgement of thanks, as his benevolent conduct merited.[4]

This 'acknowledgement' took the form of a tea set, bearing the Arms of the Garland family, complete with Crest—in colour.[5] (Of this tea set, only a single cup survives.) As for the quarrymen, they were rewarded with the sum of one guinea apiece.[6]

Next day, 10 January, *The Times* newspaper published further, harrowing details of *Halsewell*'s final moments.

> The youngest daughter [Mary Ann]... was dead in her father's arms before Mr. Meriton quitted the ship; he offered an orange to the eldest [Eliza], which she accepted and eat [ate] part of. Mr Schultz, it is supposed, could have escaped, but his attachment to the young Ladies, with whom he was but newly acquainted, prevented him from using the necessary exertions for self-preservation.[7]

*   *   *   *   *

What, if anything, survived of the fabric of the good ship *Halsewell*, with her elegant cutwater,[8] majestic sterncastle, and ornately carved taffrail (i.e. railing around deck of sterncastle)?

> A quantity of the wreckage was brought to Newton Manor [Swanage]. One of the ship's trucks [gun carriages] being hung in the hall as a memento. Some of the timbers went into the construction of a cart shed on Newton Farm.

Also, a fragment of the ship's timber was used to make an inkstand.[9] Subsequently, over the years, many other interesting and intriguing artefacts would be retrieved, as will shortly be seen.

Salvaging the wreck

A letter from a correspondent in Weymouth, dated 14 January 1786, eight days after *Halsewell* struck the rocks, was published in the *Hampshire Chronicle*. It read as follows.

The very severe weather has prevented any experiments being made hitherto upon the wreck of the *Halsewell*, East Indiaman, but as the place is marked by buoys etc., and the property on board her valuable, the divers will be at work as soon as the Spring approaches.

It was subsequently stated by that newspaper's reporter that

... divers from Weymouth had been able to visit the site, and with little or no equipment managed to recover a substantial amount of material. The probable technique used in their diving operations was to jump from a boat into the water possibly with a heavy weight which could easily be released. Then by holding their breath they would be able to fix the ropes onto the objects enabling the men in the boat to raise same.

From our own experience on the site, these recovery operations would have been quite simple to perform, although without the comfort of wetsuits it is unlikely that the divers could have remained in the water for longer than several hours each day.[10]

In that same month of January, it was reported that customs officers

... were able to salve from the wreck... 54 barrels of foreign red wine, three trunks of stationery, three half bend tanned hides [half of a cattle hide, obtained by dividing the skin along the line of the backbone], five partly full hogsheads [cask containing liquids, each of about 50 gallons capacity] of porter and a quantity of nails, hoops and sundry other articles of ironware.[11]

Amazingly enough, two centuries later, a wine bottle with its contents—a red-coloured liquid—still *in situ*, was salvaged from the wreck.

Later that year, the *Hampshire Chronicle* published the following advertisement.

POOLE*, Dorset,—to be sold at Auction at the Old Antelope Inn, by Joseph Rule, at two o'clock in the afternoon on Thursday 21st December, 1786, the following ARTICLES being part of the CARGO of the *HALSEWELL* EAST INDIAMAN

*Poole—a port with harbour, situated 10 miles or so to the north of where the shipwreck occurred.

Items included in the sale were:

Copper	98 loose plates
Lead	169 pigs, nine ½ pigs, 3 rolls
Anchors	3 of 18 cwt., to 25 cwt.
Iron Hoops	35 bundles, and some loose
Buoy Chains	3 of 5 to 7½ cwt.
Cast Iron	105 pigs
Carriage Guns	Twelve 9 and one 6 pounder
Spanish Hides	54
Porter	4 Hogsheads
Iron Oven	One

Included amongst other 'sundry articles' were stationery, whiting (ground chalk, used for whitewashing or cleaning metal plate), turpentine, cordage, nails, broken muskets, and bridles. These items had all been

> ... saved from the wreck of the *Halsewell* East Indiaman lately lost near St. Albans [St Aldhelm's Head], within the limits of the Port of Poole. The goods may be viewed three days before the sale by applying at the Customs House.[12]

In the 1868 edition of the Reverend John Hutchins's *The History and Antiquities of the County of Dorset*, it was reported that, eight decades after the loss of *Halsewell*, 'portions of the ship's timbers and copper are from time to time cast up, or discovered wedged in the rocks...'.[13] This was presumably a reference to copper plate, which as already mentioned, the HEIC exported to the East Indies for use in the construction of its ships. However, the presence of such 'loose plates' of copper suggests that the hull of *Halsewell* herself may, in part at least, have been, 'copper-bottomed'—i.e. sheathed in sheets of copper.

The Human Toll

According to Meriton

> All those who reached the summit survived, except two or three, who are supposed to have expired in drawing up [i.e. in being hauled up the cliff by rope], and a black [presumably a lascar], who died in a few hours after he was brought to the house [i.e. Eastington], though many of them were so miserably bruised that their lives were doubtful, and they are scarcely yet recovered.[14]

A stile (arrangement of steps permitting people, but not animals, to enter or leave a field) subsequently became known as 'Black Man's Gate'.

It is believed that the majority of the dead from *Halsewell* were buried at Seacombe Bottom—the lower part of Seacombe Valley—that a cross was erected here by local quarrymen, and that cannon recovered from the ship— which have long since disappeared—were placed here to mark the site. In 1856, seven decades later, it was stated that

> on the little patch of flat ground where the cliffs divide, and the stream, when there is a stream, descends to the sea, may yet be seen the traces of four long graves.[15]

On 10 January 1786, it was reported in *The Times* newspaper that

> The body of the unfortunate Capt. Peirce, has been found at Christchurch [then in Hampshire], near twenty miles from [east of] Purbeck, where some part of the wreck has also floated on shore. The widow, at the time of receiving the shocking intelligence, which was imparted in the most tender manner by Capt. Hammet [probably a reference to William Hammett, Captain of the East Indiaman *Ponsborne*], was suckling her youngest daughter, and had just time and recollection sufficient to give the infant to an attendant ere she sunk lifeless on the floor: she has remained ever since in a situation too dreadful for description.[16]

News of the *Halsewell* disaster reached as far as Scotland, when, on 12 January 1786, *The Scots Magazine* published this letter, from a resident of Christchurch.

> Every day brings in fresh intelligence of dead bodies being cast on shore on the west beach, from the wreck of the unfortunate *Halsewell* Indiaman. There were two buried here yesterday, and two more are to be buried this day; and I heard last night four or five dead bodies were lying on the beach. The foreshore from Christ Church head to Poole, is strewn with wreck.[17]

Said a correspondent, in a letter to the *Hampshire Chronicle*, dated 21 January 1786

> The unfortunate Mrs. Peirce has not been able to quit her bed, since the melancholy tale has been unfolded to her; at present there is little hope of her surviving this severe shock of Providence.[18]

Christchurch Priory's burial records reveal that Captain Peirce's daughter Mary, 'was found drowned at the West Cliff on the 21 January 1786',[19] and that three days previously, the body of Elizabeth Blackburn (mistakenly registered as 'Mrs') had been discovered, washed ashore in the same vicinity.[20] Both were buried in the Priory graveyard. The fact of these two young ladies being united in death as they had once been in life, is truly one of heartrending poignancy.

On 13 February 1786, the *Hampshire Chronicle*, which had earlier confirmed the report of Captain Peirce's body having been found, now retracted it, saying

A Correspondent who has lately been at Christchurch corrects a paragraph in our former paper, respecting the body of the unfortunate Captain Peirce, of the *Halsewell*, being found and buried there: he not having yet been found.

Having been tormented by such conflicting reports, as to the fate of her husband, Mary Peirce now faced the prospect of life without not only him, but also her two daughters, her brother, and her late husband's two nieces.

Worth Matravers' burial register for the year 1786 recorded the burial, on 15 February, of 'a man lost with the *Halsewell* East Indiaman'.[21]

Meanwhile, Christchurch's burial records for 1786 contain the following entries. 12 January: 'A person drownd [*sic*] at the West Cliff'. The following day, it was stated that Midshipman Charles Webber and [passenger] Mr. John George Schultz, 'out of the *HALSWELL* [*sic*] Indiaman & 3 others their names unknown' were also 'found drownd'. On 14 January another five drowned men were discovered; on 26 January two more men; on 29th, a man and a woman, and on 30th, a man.[22] However, according to the *Hampshire Chronicle*, a total of

... about twenty bodies have been found and buried there [at Christchurch] with the greatest decency and respect—Those who have not been owned, and whose friends do not appear to bury them, are interred at the expense of the Lord of the Manor, G. I. Tapps, who humanely stood forth on this occasion.[23]

Captain Thomas was at sea at the time of the *Halsewell* disaster, and it was only four months later, when he returned from China, that he learnt of the loss of his son William, the ship's Fifth Mate, 'a boy of sixteen'.[24] The tombstones of Elizabeth Blackburn and Charles Webber still survive in the churchyard of Christchurch Priory, though their inscriptions have been largely worn away by the passage of time. In addition to those victims referred to above,

Meriton singled out the following for special mention. James Brimer, the supernumerary Fifth Mate, was a

> Gentleman who had only been married nine days before the ship sailed, to a beautiful lady, the daughter of Capt. Norman, of the Royal Navy, in which service Mr. Brimer was a lieutenant, but was now on a voyage to visit an uncle in Madras....

Although Brimer managed to reach the cavern

> ... where he remained till the morning, when he crawled out, and a rope being thrown to him, he was either so benumbed with the cold as to fasten it about him improperly, or so agitated, as to neglect making it fast at all; but from which ever cause it arose, the effect was fatal to him; at the moment of his supposed preservation, he fell from his stand, and was unfortunately dashed to pieces, in the presence of those who could only lament the deplorable fate of an amiable and worthy man, and an able and skilful officer.[25]

James and his brother William, both midshipmen aboard *Halsewell*, were the sons of the Reverend Francis Humphries, curate of Hampstead. They were last seen 'by one of the seamen, aiding each other in the devouring waves, but we are unhappy not to find their names in the list of survivors'. One of the Reverend's pupils, 'a young gentleman, whose name is Lewis', was also a friend of his two sons. Lewis's 'distress on hearing the horrid tale [of *Halsewell*] was truly fraternal', so much so that he

> ... could scarcely refrain from... exploring the coast for the recovery of their bodies, to perform his last kind office; by their decent internment.[26]

Of their fellow midshipman Thomas Jeane, Meriton declared

> ... his fate was also attended with many calamitous circumstances; after he had quitted the ship and gained a rock, he was again swept off by the devouring waves, swimming well he a second time got footing on the rock, but being now worn out with fatigue, and stiff with cold, he could not support himself against the continued assaults of the tempest, but after seven hours endurance of all the discomforts of his situation, he was compelled by debility to abandon his only hope of life and perished in the sea.[27]

Midshipman Charles Beckford Templer was also lost, and an ornate marble tablet in his memory may be seen in the Church of St Peter & St Paul, Teingrace, Devonshire. Finally, said Meriton

... the destiny of a drummer belonging to the military on board the *Halsewell*, was attended with circumstances of peculiar distress; being either washed off the rock by the seas, or falling into the surf from above, he was carried by the counter seas on returning waves, beyond the breakers, within which his utmost efforts could never again bring him, but he was drawn further out to sea, and as he swam remarkably well, continued to struggle with the waves, in sight of his pitying companions, till his strength was exhausted, and he sunk, to rise no more.[28]

The last will and testament of Henry Pilcher, *Halsewell's* Fourth Mate, who did not survive the shipwreck, makes for sad reading.

First and principally I recommend my soul unto the hand of Almighty God hoping for remission of all my sins through the merits of Jesus Christ my beloved Saviour and Redeemer.... I give and bequeath unto my dear sister Onoria Pilcher all sure wages Sum and Sums of money as now is or hereafter shall be due to me for my service or otherwise on board the said ship....

Witnesses to the will were W. Raymer (unidentified), and Henry Meriton and John Rogers 'of the *Halsewell*'.[29]

*   *   *   *   *

In 1894, *Halsewell's* hourglass, the function of which was to time the period of the ship's watch, was donated to Dorset's County Museum, having been found washed ashore on a cushion of seaweed. The colour of its glass was green, and it was mounted in a protective wooden frame with octagonal top and base, 13 inches in height and 21 inches in width.

Analysis of the Disaster: Was Captain Peirce in Any Way to Blame?

In a letter to *The Gentleman's Magazine*, dated 21 January 1786, a person known only by his initials 'P.H.J.' of Christchurch, Hampshire questioned the competence of Captain Peirce, and the loyalty of his crew. Before addressing the specific questions asked by the correspondent, it is instructive to reconstruct *Halsewell*'s final moments, but in the absence of a surviving ship's log, this reconstruction has, of necessity, to be based largely on the account provided by Henry Meriton, her Second Mate.

When *Halsewell* sailed through The Downs on Sunday 1 January 1786 and onwards into the Dover Strait, she would undoubtedly have chosen a time to do so when the tide was most favourable. In the English Channel, there is a regular, periodic ebbing and flowing of the tides, and it is in the Dover Strait, where the Channel is at its narrowest, that these tides flow most strongly,

Ideally, *Halsewell* would have positioned herself at the entrance to the Dover Strait at between 4 a.m. and 5 a.m. on the morning of Monday 2 January, when the tide had just turned and was beginning to flow in a south-westerly direction. Over the next 4 hours, this so-called 'ebb tide' would gain in strength, reaching a maximum speed of about 2.2 knots, before gradually slackening until it changed direction again at between 9 a.m. and 10 a.m., when the reverse, 'flood tide' commenced to flow from the south west. By this time, *Halsewell* would have cleared the strait, and reached a position where the channel broadens out, and therefore where a), the influence of the tidal stream (now incoming) was less pronounced and b), the opportunities for avoiding its full force, for example, by keeping out of the main stream and sailing closer to the shore were greater. Finally, when the ebb tide resumed at between 4 p.m. and 5 p.m., *Halsewell* would be able to take full advantage of it.[1]

On that morning of Monday 2 January, Meriton reported that the weather was calm, though he made no mention of what the strength and direction of the wind was at this time. But since the journey from The Downs into the English Channel and thence towards the Isle of Wight appears to have passed off uneventfully, it is assumed that it was not unfavourable.

The intention that afternoon was to land the pilot on the Isle of Wight, as was the custom. However, the breeze being unreliable ('baffling'), and with snow falling thickly and freezing, *Halsewell*'s sails could not be furled, so further progress down channel became impossible. Captain Peirce was therefore obliged, at 9 p.m., to drop anchor—presumably at the western entrance to the Solent—the waterway which leads to Southampton Water and thence to the port of Southampton. However, on Tuesday 3rd at 4 a.m., when *Halsewell* had lain at anchor for 7 hours or so, a 'strong gale' blew up from east-north-east. The elements now took charge, and she was driven out to sea.

The intention now was to continue the voyage westward, but at 8 p.m. there came a strengthening wind from the south, which by 10 p.m. had become a 'violent gale'. This threatened to drive *Halsewell* ashore. She now began shipping water through her hawse holes: the hawse plugs having failed. However, when the ship's well was sounded, this revealed an even more serious problem. Her hull had sprung a leak, and her hold now contained water to a depth of 5 feet. This would cause the ship to sail lower in the water, and therefore less efficiently. Also, the height of her freeboard (the part of the ship's side between the water line and the deck) would be reduced, making her more vulnerable to waves washing over her, thus imperilling her further. Furthermore, in the face of the violent gale, *Halsewell* was more likely to heel, and thereby ship even more water.

At 2 a.m. on Wednesday 4th, Peirce found that he was unable to manoeuvre the ship (in this instance by gybing). He accordingly ordered that the mizzen mast be 'cut away', presumably to prevent her a), from heeling and b), from being driven onshore. (The mizzen sails accounted for some 15 per cent of the ship's total of approximately 13,000 square feet of sail). However, *Halsewell* continued to sink still lower, her pumps being unable to keep pace with the rate of ingress of water into her hold. Aware that she was 'in immediate danger of foundering'—i.e. filling up with water and sinking—Captain Peirce now made an even more drastic decision: to cut away the main mast (which carried some 50 per cent of her total area of sail).

At 8 a.m., Peirce succeeded in manoeuvring *Halsewell* so that she was 'before the wind'. Therefore, assuming that it was continuing to blow from the south, she was now sailing northwards. Furthermore, during this time the action of the pumps had reduced the level of water in the hold by 2 feet. With only the foresail (the principal sail on the foremast which, under normal conditions, accounted for only 7 per cent of her total square footage of sail) still operational, Captain Peirce now pointed his ship eastwards. At 10 a.m. there came a further blow to *Halsewell*'s sailing capability, when the fore topmast came crashing down, destroying the foresail in the process.

At 11 a.m., with the wind now coming from the west, a new foresail was 'bent', and a jury mainmast erected, using a top gallant sail for a mainsail. As already mentioned, even under normal circumstances a sailing ship such as *Halsewell* was capable of making little progress against a prevailing wind, and in her present crippled state, probably none at all. She therefore had no alternative but to sail eastward, before the wind, towards Portsmouth and the protection of the Mother Bank.

Had the wind continued from the west, then all might have been well, but on Thursday 5 January at 2 a.m., it commenced to blow 'fresh' from the south, and by 8 p.m., a 'strong' southerly gale was blowing. Captain Peirce then 'wore the ship'—i.e. gybed, so that she was pointing westward, but finding that she was now losing ground, he gybed again in order that she should now 'stretch on' in an easterly direction.

However, to make matters worse, between 7 p.m. and 8 p.m., the tide turned and the new flood tide began to surge up the channel at an ever increasing rate, reaching a maximum speed of 2.0 knots at 10 p.m., and continuing to flow in a north-easterly direction until 2 a.m. the following morning. From 11 p.m., when *Halsewell* was a mere 1½ miles south of St Aldhelm's Head, and for the next 2 hours it would swirl fiercely around the headland, vortex-like in an anti-clockwise direction (the so-called 'St Aldhelm's race'). This was guaranteed to propel the ship even further towards the rocky shore to the east,[2] and in particular the rocky ledge, which extends out to sea in a south-westerly direction from St Aldhelm's Head. This ledge gives rise to overfalls—turbulent stretches of open water caused by a strong current or tide running over a submarine ridge[3]—which can extend from between 3.5 and 5 miles offshore.

At 11 p.m., Captain Peirce resorted to the only option left to him: the bower anchor was lowered to arrest *Halsewell*'s progress. This, however, was effective for only about an hour, when once again, she was driven by the wind. The same procedure was now employed using the sheet anchor, which was effective in holding her only for another two hours or so, when she 'drove again'. Finally, the long battle against the elements was lost, and shortly after 2 a.m. on the morning of Friday 6 January, *Halsewell*, despite having rounded ('weathered') St Aldhelm's Head, foundered upon the rocky shore, a mile or so to the east.

*   *   *   *   *

The aforementioned letter written by 'P.H.J.' to the *Gentleman's Magazine* is now reproduced here, with the author of this account's comments inserted below each point raised.

> *The following questions are submitted to the consideration of any reader of your useful Miscellany, who has it in his power to answer them, respecting the dreadful accident which lately befell the unfortunate Halsewell outward bound East Indiaman, the circumstances attending which, being so peculiarly distressing, have diffused a general gloom amongst all ranks of people, except indeed the rapacious plunderers on the sea coast, who are so devoid of humanity as to strip the bodies of the dead as soon as the waves have thrown them on the shore: which, however, some gentlemen in the vicinity of this place, to their honour let it be spoken, have had decently interred.*
>
> *Question 1. As the ship, during the violent snow storm of the 4th instant, had her main and mizen masts cut away, and several feet of water in the hold, why did not the captain, after the weather became moderate, make for the first leeward port, and put into Plymouth?*

In the face of a westerly wind, there was no way that *Halsewell*, in her stricken state, could have reached the safety of Plymouth, situated as it is, 30 miles or so to the west of Berry Head.

> *Question 2. When the ship came to anchor off Portland, in a second storm early in the morning of the 6th instant, why was not the foremast immediately cut away, which probably might have prevented the ship from driving on the rocks, where, in ten minutes, she was dashed to pieces?*

Here, Mr Urban is incorrect in his chronology. By the early morning of 6 January, *Halsewell* had rounded St Aldhelm's Head and was caught up in the St Aldhelm's Race. Therefore, cutting away the foremast (and jury mainsail) could only have served to prolong the inevitable.

> *Question 3. Whether there is any truth in the report circulated in the public papers, that the ship's crew refused to do their duty? And, if they did, from what cause such refusal proceeded?*

The mutinous behaviour of *Halsewell*'s ordinary seamen has already been described, and a possible explanation for it given.

Queſtion IV.   What is the meaning of the ſhip's name, the Halſewell †?

† It is the name of the feat of Sir Charles Kemys Tynte, bart. in Somerſetſhire, who probably was a conſiderable owner.   EDIT.

Extract from the *Gentleman's Magazine*.

Question 4. What is the meaning of the ship's name, the Halsewell?

This will be revealed shortly.

If either of the surviving officers, or any other of the parties concerned, will take the trouble to answer the above in your next Magazine, it will have a tendency to vindicate the captain's conduct of [alleged] imprudence: and, on that account will, I hope, be agreeable to your readers in general, and will particularly oblige, Yours P.H.J.[4]

The question is, was Captain Peirce in any way responsible for the loss of his ship? There were others, besides Meriton, who attested to just how atrocious the conditions were in that first week of January 1786. For example, T. H. Baker (who subsequently became a Fellow of the Meteorological Society of London), in his private 'weather diary' for that year, stated as follows

January 3rd, at night and the next morning, the severest gale of wind ever remembered, wind S.S.E. to S. The damage done to the shipping at Plymouth is almost incredible. Heavy thunder and dreadful lightning all the night at Falmouth [south west Cornwall]. For several days previous there was very hard frosts.

   The violence of the wind was so great on 3rd that the roof of Gloucester Cathedral sustained great damage. Ten tons of lead was torn up and rolled together. The *Halsewell* East Indiaman... after experiencing several hard gales of wind with an uncommonly heavy fall of snow was lost on 6th off the Purbeck.[5]

HCS *Ganges*, *Halsewell*'s companion during her final voyage, would have encountered the same stormy conditions. How did she fare? Fortunately, not only did she survive, her (logbook—*Journal*) has been preserved, and it is this which may provide the answer.[6] According to her captain James Williamson, on 1 November 1785, *Ganges* 'hauled out of Greenland Dock & dropt down to Deptford'. On 21 November, she arrived at Gravesend, along with East Indiamen *Manship* and *Halsewell* herself. On 31 December, as *Ganges* lay at anchor off the Nore—a sandbank at the mouth of the Thames, marked by a lighted buoy—'came down the *Halsewell* East Indiaman & anchored close to us'. At 8 a.m. the following morning, 1 January 1786, *Ganges* set sail.

At noon on 2 January, when *Ganges* was '6 or 7 Leagues'—about 20 nautical miles—off Dunnose (Isle of Wight), Williamson recorded in his log, '*Halsewell* in Coy [company]'. On the morning of 3 January, he wrote, 'Hard Squalls with a great deal of snow', and later that day, 'Several Sail in Sight'. However, there was no subsequent mention of *Halsewell*. The following morning there were, 'Hard Gales with Heavy Squalls, Rain & Hail'. In 'getting down' the top gallant yards, the top gallant sail 'blew loose & split'. At 5 p.m. on 5 January, Berry Head (a landmark which *Halsewell* had sighted at 11 a.m. the previous day) was in sight. Said Williamson

> Having met with much bad Wear [weather] & the People [crew] falling sick, at 8 [p.m.] Bore away for St Helens [east coast of Isle of Wight] made Portland the Wind Shifting was forced to Tack to clear it.

At 2 a.m. on the morning of 6 January, and unbeknown to Captain Williamson, *Halsewell* had struck the rocks near Seacombe. Meanwhile, *Ganges*' captain reported

> Fresh Gales with Squalls & Rain thick Weather throughout & a Heavy Sea coming in find it Impossible to clear Portland or the Start [Start Point] on either Tack.

Nevertheless, *Ganges* <u>did</u> manage to round Portland, for on 8 January, Captain Williamson recorded that she was 'abreast of Dunnose'. Here a pilot sloop was encountered, whereupon the pilot Mr Cooper, came aboard and 'took charge of the ship'. She subsequently found a safe anchorage at Portsmouth's Mother Bank, where, on 10 January, 'Caulkers' set about 'Caulking the Quick Work [probably the hull above the water line] on ye Starboard Side'. *Ganges* finally set sail again, completed her voyage to Coast and Bay, and returned safely to The Downs on 26 July 1787.[7]

Clearly, like *Halsewell*, *Ganges* was blown back up the Channel by the force of the wind, sustained structural damage—hence the recaulking—

though not on the same scale as *Halsewell*—and almost failed to round Portland, in which case it is likely that she would have suffered the same fate as her companion.

In further defence of Captain Peirce, it was reported that

Out of a fleet of 13 sail of Swedish merchant ships, laden with stores consigned for l'Orient, in France, two only have reached their destined port, the other eleven having been wrecked in that heavy gale of wind in which the *Halsewell* perished.[8]

'Halsewell':
From Whence Did
the Ship Derive her Name?

The question, 'What is the meaning of the ship's name, the *Halsewell*?' was posed by a contributor to the *Gentleman's Magazine* in 1786, the year in which the shipwreck occurred. To this, the magazine's editor responded as follows

> It is the name of the seat of Sir Charles Kemys [Kemeys] Tynte, bart. [Baronet] in Somersetshire, who probably was a considerable owner.[1]

This was a reference to Halswell* House, Sir Charles's country mansion and estate in the parish of Goathurst in Somerset. (*The discrepancy in the spelling of the name will be discussed shortly.)

When it came to choosing the name of an East Indiaman on, or prior to her launch, this was normally the prerogative of its managing owner—in this instance Thomas Burston, Esquire. In the case of *Halsewell*, as Sir Charles was 'a considerable owner'—i.e. owner of a share in the ship herself, and/or a share in the enterprise—then this would account for the choice of name.

From whence did the name 'Halswell' derive? Prior to the Norman Conquest of 1066, it is recorded that the Manor of Halswell was occupied by one Alweard. According to the Domesday Book (record of a survey of England carried out in 1086 by officials of William the Conqueror), 'Wido held it [owned, or was a tenant] of Roger of Arundel', and by 1280, Peter of Halswell held the manor.[2] In fact, the Halswell dynasty was subsequently associated with the Manor of Halswell for almost seven centuries. As for the manor house

In 1318, William de Halswell obtained a licence to have mass said in his own oratory in his house, then called Halswell Court. Nothing remains to be seen of that medieval manor house, for in the 1530s, Nicholas Halswell [at about this time, the prefix 'de' was evidently dispensed with] built his mansion house using his inheritance from his step-father and father-in-law John Tremayle of Blackmoor, Cannington [Somersetshire]. This was probably a modest Tudor courtyard house which was further extended by his grandson Sir Nicholas Halswell.

The east, south and part of the north range of this [sixteenth century] house still survive... but the remaining part of the north range was demolished to make way for the grand new 3-storey, 7-bayed north range, probably built by William Taylor of London for Sir Halswell Tynte [1st Baronet] and bearing the date 1689.[3]

What was the relationship between Sir Charles Kemeys-Tynte and the Halswell family? Sir Charles's great-grandfather was John Tynte (1617-1669) of Chelvey, Somerset, who, during the Civil Wars (1642-1648), served as colonel in command of Royalist troops. In about 1645, John married Jane Halswell (1629-1650), daughter of the Reverend Hugh Halswell, Rector of Cheriton, Hampshire and Proctor of Oxford University, and his wife Millicent née Test. Thus were the Tynte and Halswell families united. Jane bore John a son, Halswell Tynte (1649-1702).[4]

Members of the family spelt their surname 'Halswell'—viz. the inscriptions on their tombstones in Goathurst's parish church—yet the name of the family seat was sometimes spelt 'Halsewell'—for example, by Sir Bernard Burke in his *A Genealogical and Heraldic History of the Landed Gentry of Great Britain and Northern Ireland*, published in 1863.[5] The two spellings may therefore be regarded as interchangeable, this accounts for the fact that the ship which is the subject of this account, was given the name 'Halsewell', and not 'Halswell'.

To return to Sir Charles Kemys Tynte. In 1736 he married Ann Busby of Addington, Buckinghamshire. There were no offspring of the marriage. Three years later, in 1740, he succeeded his brother John, as 5th Baronet and inherited the family seat Halswell House, and its estate Halswell Park. In 1745, Sir Charles was elected MP for Monmouth, and from 1747-1774 he served as MP for Somerset (a parliamentary constituency which returned two Members of Parliament). It was he would make the greatest impact on both manor house and estate, as will shortly be seen.

Sir Charles Kemeys-Tynte re-modelled the west front to the designs of master builder and architect Francis Cartwright, and built two bay windows and a tall screen with ornamental niches across the service court. He also carried out alterations to the interior.[6]

J. Richards R. A.: Halswell, in Somersetshire, the seat of Sir Charles Kemeys Tynte, Bart, *c.* 1788.

The outcome was that art historian Nikolaus Pevsner, described Halswell House as 'the most important house of its date in the country'. Pevsner, who was particularly impressed with its interior, stated that the house contained 'an excellent large square open-well staircase with strong, twisted balusters. The ceiling here and in other rooms has good plaster-work, partly of the Jones-Wren type with wreathed circles or ovals, partly with the later, daintier motifs of intertwined branches and thin trails. Excellent contemporary wooden chimneypieces'.[7] This was a reference to classical architect Inigo Jones and architect Christopher Wren.

Sir Charles also excelled in his creation of the estate 'park', with its 'classical bridge' complete with 'two strange statues at each end'; 'Druid's Temple'; 'mock ruin of a mediaeval arch'; 'ornate water cistern surmounted by a pyramid topped with a gryphon'; 'Doric Rotunda'; 'Robin Hood's hut'; 'classical temple', and 'strange monument to a much-loved horse'. Having purchased a considerable acreage of adjacent land, he removed hedges and converted arable fields to parkland. He also extended the park, 'planting trees in aesthetically pleasing places, stocking it with deer and cattle and designing his ridings [paths designed for horse-riding] so that he and his visitors could enjoy the near and distant views, the contrast between light and shade and between running and still waters'. The creation of this 'great open space' was completed in 1764.

This endeavour coincided with the heyday of Lancelot 'Capability' Brown (1715-1783), a pupil of architect William Kent, a founder of the new English style of landscape garden, recognisable for its romantic and informal style. Sir Charles's final project was the laying out of the great kitchen garden.[8]

Not surprisingly, Halswell Park, Sir Charles's extravaganza, was a magnet for the rich and famous: among them William Gilpin, clergyman, writer, and artist; Henry Hawkins Tremayne, Cornish tin-mining magnate; Horace Walpole, 4th Earl of Orford, MP and writer. Artists recorded Halswell Manor for posterity, notably John Inigo Richards, landscape painter and a founder member of the Royal Academy, whose oil on canvas 'Halswell House, Somerset' was created in 1764 (of which an etching and engraving was made), and Lady Elizabeth Lee, who made a pen-and-ink drawing of the 'medieval arch' and statue of Neptune in 1758. As for Sir Charles, he himself was painted by Henry Spurrier Parkman and by Thomas Frye.

Finally, what is the origin of the name 'Halsewell' itself? 'Halse' is Old English for 'a neck of land' (the relevance of which, in this context is admittedly obscure), and 'well', which can mean 'a spring of water rising to the surface of the earth'.9 In fact, since time immemorial there has been such a spring within the grounds of Halswell Manor. It arises in Mill Wood, where Sir Charles constructed a grotto, complete with seats and a tablet on which was inscribed the following poem

> When *Israel*'s wand'ring sons the desart trod,
> The melting rock obey'd the prophet's* rod;
> Forth gushed the stream,
> the tribes their thirst allay'd;
> Forgetful of their *God* they rose and play'd.
> Ye happy swains for whom these waters flow,
> Oh! may your hearts with grateful ardours glow;
> Lo, here a fountain streams at his command,
> Not o'er a barren, but a fruitful land;
> Where Nature's choicest gifts the vallies fill,
> And smiling Plenty gladdens ev'ry hill.

*A reference to Moses, Hebrew prophet of the *Old Testament*.

Furthermore, Sir Charles arranged for the water from this spring to descend through a series of lakes and cascades.[10] Another spring arises in the grounds adjacent to the east side of the manor house.

The 1960s:
Renewed Interest in the Wreck:
Intriguing Artefacts.

In the 1960s there was a sudden surge of interest in *Halsewell* by the diving community: first, by brothers Dennis and Bob Wright, and Bob Campbell of Swanage.[1] Since then, those who have dived on her have been rewarded, perhaps beyond their wildest expectations, by the wealth and variety of artefacts recovered. However, such operations were not without their difficulties, as Bob Errington explains. Some artefacts were discovered lying 'loose in the shale'. Also, it was necessary to 'prize from the seabed sections of concretion'. This was done using sledgehammers and chisels. Finally, in order to access these artefacts, 'large boulders have to be moved'.

Errington describes how, between the base of the cliff and 30 metres out to sea, the depth of water is from 0 to about 3-4 metres. 'You are diving down between large boulders. The tops of these boulders can be just below the surface. Out to about 50 to 70 metres the seabed drops away to about 10 metres in depth to what we call the shale area. After that it is scattered boulders and shale'.[2]

The boulders referred to are, as already mentioned, the result of numerous falls of rock from the cliffs, which have occurred in the intervening years since the shipwreck.

Wally Hammond describes how, in those days, simply reaching the wreckage was a strenuous exercise in logistics. Having left his motor car at Seacombe quarry, he and his fellow divers would load their equipment into 'a trolley made from light but strong bamboo and pram wheels. Gravity would get us the 1¼ miles down to the sea but we would have to pull it back up the hill on our return'.

And Hammond's son Keith, describes how, as a child, he played in the rock pools at Seacombe, as his father and fellow divers, led by Robin Pingree.

They would swim 'out to the caves and the wreck site, towing 6 or 7 air tanks floating on rubber rings behind them. "How much easier it would have been with boats!", he remarked.'

The 'air tanks', said Wally Hammond, were, in fact, 14 metal cylinders (twelve of which were on loan from the British Army) each containing sufficient air for about 45 minutes. This meant that the divers could work for only about 6 to 7 hours a day. 'Sometimes when our cylinders were empty and we were still fit enough we would spend a few hours snorkelling down'.

The depth was about 25 to 30 feet. As for the 'rubber rings', these were 'old inner tubes' from car tyres, obtained from the local garage. The divers inflated the inner tubes, attached two cylinders to each, and then swam out to sea, towing the tubes behind them. As for their diving suits, these were home-made by the divers, using '¼ inch thick neoprene wet-suit material' which they purchased from the diving school on Swanage Pier.

Hammond acquired a German 'Robot' camera (a type manufactured by Otto Berning & Co. in Schwelm, Westphalia), which he adapted for underwater use by encasing it in Perspex, and also by fixing a Perspex pyramidal structure to the front, with a filter to exclude plankton, which would otherwise have reflected light from the flash bulb and hence spoiled the photographs. The camera had the advantage of enabling several images to be taken in the space of a few seconds.

Items washed ashore

A baby's bonnet was 'picked up on the rocks after the wreck' (i.e. shortly after the sinking). Although the Reverend Morgan Jones numbered the women aboard the ship as 15 (none of whom survived), there is no mention of there being any infants aboard ship; so it is not known for whom the bonnet was intended.[3]

A *Bible* box—in which the *Holy Bible* was kept when not in use—of carved oak and ornately decorated, is now the property of the Bugler family of Swanage. One may imagine one of the terrified passengers clutching the box and praying, but to no avail, as the ship went down. Whereupon, it floated ashore on the waves.

A side table, with single drawer and turned legs united by cross stretchers, dated from the time of William and Mary (1689-1702). Inside the drawer was a note, which read

This table was found from the shipwreck of the *Halsewell* in 1786 her Burthen was 758 tons running ashore upon the rocks during a heavy snowstorm and 168 persons being lost.

Halsewell herself

Of *Halsewell*'s fabric, what little survived included a collection of nails and screws of various sizes, including a bronze nail, 1 foot in length; a complete 'knee'—an angled piece of metal, in this case with arms each of about 4 feet in length and set at right angles, used to connect and support the ship's beams and timbers—and several fragments of knees.

Jewellery

A gold mourning ring was recovered by Colin Hobbs, which bore the inscription

ELIZ OB* 10 JUNE 1775 AE* 70

(*OB—Latin *obit*—she died: *AE—Latin *aetatis*—at the age of) indicating that it commemorated a person presumably named Elizabeth, who died on the date given aged 70 years.4 Such rings were traditionally presented by the next of kin to the family and close friends of a deceased person. It is not known to whom this ring belonged. A gold object retrieved by Wally Hammond was identified as a facet of a pendant earring; also gold mounts for pendant brooches or portrait miniatures, and a gold brooch, with four of its diamonds still *in situ*.

Personal items

A fruit knife with mother-of-pearl handle and silver blade, bore the name of the manufacturer 'John Winter', 'Sheffield 1784', John Winter & Co. being located in High Street, Sheffield, Yorkshire.5 Also, a toasting fork; straining spoon; silver fork, minus its handle, with maker's mark 'RT'—Robert Trickett & Co of Sheffield; fragments of silver shoe buckles; wooden back plates for toothbrushes; chess pieces fashioned from bone; a jewellery box, and a larger, ornately carved wooden chest.

Militaria

As already mentioned, many cannon balls have been retrieved—two dozen or so by Robin Pingree and his team of divers. One of the team was Wally Hammond, who affirmed that each and every 6.5-pound cannon ball (but

Above left: Arms of the East India Company.

Above middle and right: From *Halsewell* wreck: Spanish 8-real, collectively known as 'pieces of eight'. *Photo: Charlie Newman*

Above left: From *Halsewell* wreck: pintle and gudgeon, with spare pin. *Photo: Dorset County Museum*

Above right: From *Halsewell* wreck: uniform button from the coatee of one of the ship's officer's, possibly that of Captain Pierce himself. *Photo: Ed Cumming*

Below left: From *Halsewell* wreck: quilted grapeshot. *Photo: Northampton BS-AC*

Below middle: From *Halsewell* wreck: fragment of ship's bell, with number 'I'. *Photo: Ed Cumming*

Below right: From *Halsewell* wreck: button bearing initials 'T B' (Thomas Burston). *Photo: David J. Allen*

Walnut Tree House, rear view.

Above: Love token, dedicated to 'C. Webster', and dated 1784. On reverse, 'Success to the Halsewell' and a depiction of the ship. Photo: Reverend R. W. H. Acworth Collection, Maidstone Museum & Art Gallery

Below: From *Halsewell* wreck: pair of dividers. *Photo: David J. Allen*

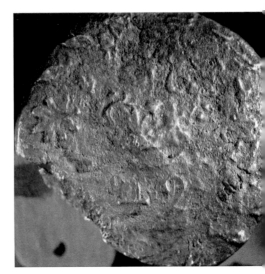

Above left: From *Halsewell* wreck: shade mounts, from a sextant. *Photo: Swanage Pier Trust*

Above right: From *Halsewell* wreck: regimental button depicting number '42' and thistle. *Photo: Wally Hammond*

East India House, by Thomas Malton the Younger (1748-1804).

Norman chapel, St Aldhelm's Head.

From *Halsewell* wreck: Thomas Burston's personal stamp and reverse. *Photo: David J. Allen*

S. W. Fores: aquatint of the Loss of *Halsewell*, published 1786. *Photo: Reproduced by permission of the Dorset History Centre*

Above: Hedbury cliff quarry (½ mile east of Seacombe), showing capstan and 'whim' (derrick-crane).

Right: Church of St Nicholas of Myra, Worth Matravers.

Below left: Tea cup, presented to the Garlands of Eastington by the Directors of the East India Company. *Photo: R. J. Saville*

Below right: Copper sheathing. Photo: *Dorset County Museum*

Above: Halsewell rock (sloping, central foreground), taken from Winspit, with Seacombe in the distance.

Below left: Halsewell: hourglass. Photo: *Dorset County Museum*

Below right: Church of St Edward King & Martyr, Goathurst, Somersetshire: Memorial to Jane Tynte, née Halswell. *Courtesy of the rector and churchwardens*

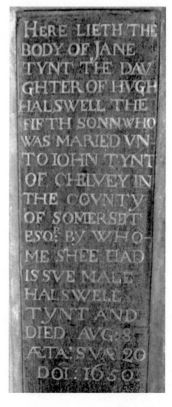

HERE LIETH THE
BODY OF IANE
TYNT THE DAV
GHTER OF HVGH
HALSWELL THE
FIFTH SONN WHO
WAS MARIED VN
TO IOHN TYNT
OF CHELVEY IN
THE COVNTY
OF SOMERSET
ESQ: BY WHO
ME SHEE HAD
ISSVE MALE
HALSWELL
TYNT AND
DIED AVG: 8
ÆTA: SVÆ 20
DOI: 1650

Church of St Edward King & Martyr: Tomb of Sir Nicholas Halswell and his wife Bridget, with the kneeling figures of their 6 sons and 3 daughters. *Courtesy of the rector and churchwardens*

Detail from the tomb in the church of St Edward King & Martyr.

SACRED to the Memory
of Sir CHARLES KEMEYS TYNTE Bart,
WHO BY THE DISCHARGE OF
the Publick and Private Duties of his Station in Life,
REFLECTED ADDITIONAL LUSTRE ON
A LONG AND NOBLE ANCESTRY.
He served his Country in Five Parliaments:
In the Four last he represented this his native County
and in 1774 retired full of HONOUR.
He married ANN, the Elder Daughter and Co-heiress of the Reverend
THOMAS BUSBY L.L.D. of Addington in the County of Bucks;
by whom, from the Affection due to
the BEST of HUSBANDS, this Monument was erected.
He died Aug.st 25th 1785; aged 76

Church of St Edward King & Martyr: Memorial to Sir Charles Kemeys-Tynte, by Joseph Nollekens. *Courtesy of the rector and churchwardens*

Above left: From *Halsewell* wreck: Bible box. *Photo: Ed Cumming*

Above right: From *Halsewell* wreck: side table. Photo: Ann & Roger Day and 15.3 Note attached to side table.

ELIZA OR ELIZABETH — - - - · DIED   10th JUNE 1775   AGED 70,

OB   ÆT.

Artist's impression of inscription on mourning ring. *Photo: Ian Carruthers*

Above left: From *Halsewell* wreck: One face of a pendant earring. *Photo: Wally Hammond*

Above right: From *Halsewell* wreck: gold brooch and surround, with six small diamonds. *Photo: Northampton BS-AC*

Above: From *Halsewell* wreck: fruit knife. Photo: *Dorset County Museum*

Below left: From *Halsewell* wreck: toasting fork and straining spoon. *Photo: David J. Allen*

Below right: From *Halsewell* wreck: silver fork with maker's mark 'RT' – Robert Trickett & Co. of Sheffield. *Photo: Northampton BS-AC*

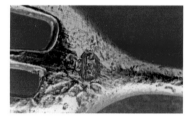

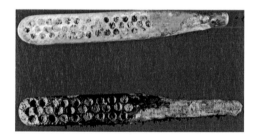

Above: From *Halsewell* wreck: wooden back-plates for brushes. *Photo: Ed Cumming*

Right: From *Halsewell* wreck: chess pieces in bone. *Photo: Ed Cumming*

Above: Flintlock musket, retrieved from the wreck by Nathan Chinchen. *Photo: Treleven Haysom*

Below: From *Halsewell* wreck: barrel of a musketoon. *Photo: Ed Cumming*

Above: Brass plaques affixed to musket. Photos: Treleven Haysom.

Left: From *Halsewell* wreck: musket 'thimbles'. *Seadart Divers Association*

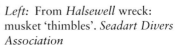

From *Halsewell* wreck: gunner's rule and thimbles. *Photo: Northampton BS-AC*

From *Halsewell* wreck: cross guard for dagger or short sword. *Photo: Ed Cumming*

Above left: From *Halsewell* wreck: fragment of chinaware marked 'Turner'. *Photo: Ed Cumming*

Above middle: From *Halsewell* wreck: water feeder for birds. *Photo: Ed Cumming*

Above right: From *Halsewell* wreck: military horse tack. *Photo: David J. Allen*

Below: From *Halsewell* wreck: three padlocks (minus their clasps). *Photo: Ed Cumming*

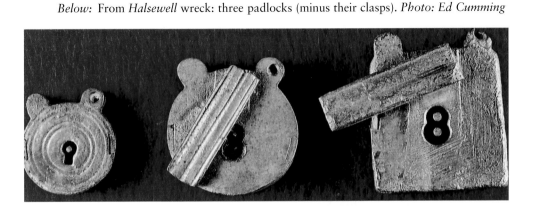

Right: From *Halsewell* wreck: assorted metalware, including musket trigger guards. *Photo: Northampton BS-AC*

Below left: From *Halsewell* wreck: furniture castor. *Photo: Swanage Pier Trust*

Below middle and right: From *Halsewell* wreck: bale token and reverse. *Photo: Northampton BS-AC*

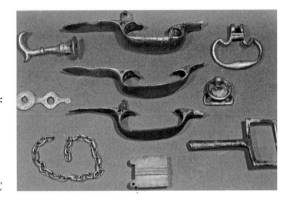

Above: From *Halsewell* wreck: George II silver shilling, dated 1758. Photo: Charlie Newman.

Right: From *Halsewell* wreck: mystery object. *Photo: Ed Cumming*

Above left: From *Halsewell* wreck: George III gold guinea, of which around thirty have been recovered. Seadart Divers Association.

Above right: From *Halsewell* wreck: Danish skilling. *Photo: David J. Allen*

Below left: From *Halsewell* wreck: wine bottle, cork inscribed 'Chatfield of London'. *Photo: Ed Cumming*

Below right: From *Halsewell* wreck: button inscribed 'GENERAL POST OFFICE' and bearing number '107'. *Photo: Seadart Divers Association*

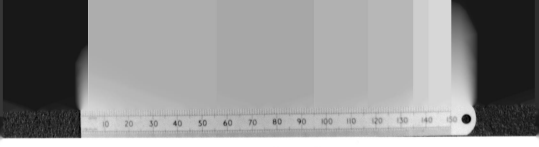

Above: From *Halsewell* wreck: glass vial. *Photo: Ed Cumming*

Below left: From *Halsewell* wreck: brass protractor, wine glasses, apothecary's cup, and jewellery box with label 'A Relic of Y late Tragedy Found at Halswell Rock'.

Below right: From *Halsewell* wreck: selection of cufflinks, including a pair depicting a balloon (top left). *Photo: Ed Cumming*

Above left: From *Halsewell* wreck: gold pocket watch, showing name of maker 'Jn Hodges', serial number '1791', and place of manufacture 'London'. *Photo: Ed Cumming*

Above right: From *Halsewell* wreck: winder key for pocket watch or small clock. *Photo: Northampton BS-AC*

Left: From *Halsewell* wreck: livery button. *Photo: Ed Cumming*

Right: From *Halsewell* wreck: chatelaine in gold. *Photo: Ed Cumming*

Above left: King George III, mezzotint portrait by Jonathan Spilsbury.

Above right: Queen Charlotte, mezzotint portrait by Jonathan Spilsbury.

Above left: Pencil drawing of J. M. W. Turner, by Cornelius Varley. *Sheffield City Art Galleries*

Above right: J. M. W. Turner, 'The Loss of an East Indiaman', watercolour, *c.* 1818. *Photo: Cecil Higgins Art Gallery & Museum, Bedford*

Above: All Saints Church, Kingston-upon-Thames, 1840. From Edward Wedlake Brayley, *A Topographical History of Surrey.* J. S. Virtue, London, 1878-81.

Below: Sword, presented to Captain Henry Meriton of Exeter by the Patriotic Fund in 1804. *Photo: courtesy of Thomas Del Mar*

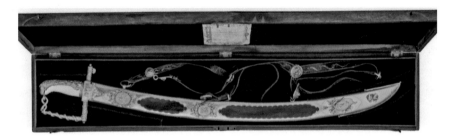

Below left: From *Halsewell* wreck: cabinet, believed to be the upper portion of a secretaire bookcase. *Photo: R. J. Saville*

Below right: From *Halsewell* wreck: mirror, Dutch, 18th century.

Above: Mourning ring, depicting the sinking *Halsewell*, and inscribed 'C. B. [Charles Beckford] Templer / Periit Jany 6 1786'. *Photo: Bristol Museum & Art Gallery*

Mourning ring, depicting a funerary urn, and inscribed 'Miss Amy Paul Aged 18 / Miss Mary Paul Aged 16 / Charles Beckford Templer, Esq. Aged 15. / Died 6th Jany. 1786. *Photo: Richard Daglish*

Below left: Miss Elizabeth Blackburn's tombstone, the churchyard, Christchurch Priory. *Photo: Jean Sutton*

Below right: Midshipman Charles Webber's tombstone, the churchyard, Christchurch Priory. *Photo: Jean Sutton*

not the 9-pound ones) had a core of lead which formed a circular disc of about 2 cm in diameter at the surface, at the point where it was exposed. Initially, he said, 'we thought that this lead plug was used to hold the end of the chain, in the case of chain shot, or the rod in the case of bar shot. However when we sliced open these lead plugs, there was no sign of any internal iron'.

Hammond subsequently saw a documentary programme on BBC Television in which the custodian of Southsea Castle, Portsmouth, produced a similar looking cannon ball. However, in this case, its disc was stamped with the monogram of King Henry VIII, indicating that he had commissioned them to be made.6 Hammond believed that, in order to obtain this impression, then the material in question must have been lead'. However, it was not possible to identify any such markings on the cannon balls from *Halsewell*.[7]

The cannon balls, together with two grenades (small bombs, thrown by hand or launched mechanically)[8] were preserved by Hammond using the technique of electrolysis.

A flintlock musket, to the forestock of which was subsequently affixed a brass plaque bearing the inscription 'Saved from the Wreck of the Halsewell Seacomb Jany 1786', and to the buttstock, a similar brass plaque inscribed with the words 'Presented to Francis Haysom by Nathan Chinchen'. Swanage fisherman and quarryman Francis Haysom was born in 1791, 5 years after the shipwreck. Nathan Chinchen was a Swanage stone merchant, who worked the Winspit and Seacombe quarries. He was also captain of the sea fencibles—soldiers belonging to the British militia which could be called up only for service on home soil.[9] Francis Haysom's father William was also a member of the sea fencibles, and probably served under Chinchen.[10] As it could not possibly have floated ashore, and given the dire circumstances of the shipwreck, it is virtually certain that the aforesaid musket was recovered by a diver. An opinion on the musket was sought from the Royal Armouries Museum, Leeds, Yorkshire, which is as follows.

> The style of the lock is undoubtedly French, with the heart-shaped throat hole, cheese-headed screws on the sideplate, and the brass pan. The trigger and trigger guard are also in the French style, as is the brass barrel band. The flint held in the jaws of the cock appears to have been knapped in the French 'Wedge' style. The colour of the flint also looks correct for a French piece of flint (rather than a British one).

However, the musket does not match any French army or naval musket of the period, and it is therefore not a military piece. According to the Royal Armouries Museum

The fact that it is half stocked [i.e. the stock extends only half the length of the barrel] suggests that it is a sporting firearm.[11]

The probability is, therefore, that the musket belonged to one of the passengers. The significance of the 'S' and '8' (or '? 'B') carved into the stock is, together with 11 punched indentations, is not clear. Finally, how did a French musket come to be aboard a British ship. Who knows? (The Anglo-French War, which had commenced in 1778, had terminated in 1783, three years prior to *Halsewell*'s demise.)

Also, musket thimbles, which were fitted to the underside of the barrel of such weapons to house the ramrod; the barrel of a musketoon (short-barrelled version of the musket), and a gunner's rule, which enabled the gunner to select the appropriate shot and powder charge to use, once he had measured the calibre of his gun. Also, a pommel, once part of a dagger. It is likely that this weapon had once belonged to one of the midshipman, rather than to a soldier of the 42nd Regiment of Foot—whose 'dirks' were of a less intricate design.

Pottery

A pottery plate bears the maker's mark 'Turner'. This was John Turner (1738-87), manufacturer of high quality, white, Staffordshire stoneware pottery; first at Stoke on Trent, and subsequently at nearby Lane End. In 1784, Turner was appointed Potter to the Prince of Wales.

It has been suggested that a pottery vessel with a projecting spout near its base, may have been a 'bird feeder'—i.e. a dispenser for bird seed, the keeping of caged birds being in vogue at that time. Also, items of creamware from a dinner service included the leg of a tureen.

Pewter

Of some two dozen pewter spoons, some are inscribed on the back with the letter 'X', but otherwise, no maker's marks survive. Four tiny pewter taps, each with a bore of about ⊠ inch, may have belonged to pewter cisterns into which wine was decanted.

Metalware

Two finials were recovered: one in the shape of a pineapple contained in a vase, and the other in the shape of a bird with outstretched wings. Also, several brass padlocks, minus their hasps, which, being made of iron, had corroded away; a large hasp (hinged metal fastening fitted over a loop and secured by a pin), the function of which is not known; a key; fragment of a horse brass; coat hooks; fittings for furniture ware, including hinges, door handles, and castors with leather wheels which still revolved.

A bale token, inscribed with the letters 'VEIC' ('United East India Company'). The device in the shape of the number '4' is barely discernible, is believed to represent the Christian cross, though disguised in order to avoid causing offence to non-Christians. The ring at the top is missing. Through the ring, the token would have been fastened to items such as bales of cloth, by means of a split pin.

Coinage

Many silver Spanish eight-real coins (alternatively known as 'dollars' or 'pieces of eight') were recovered; some bearing the letter 'M' with a small circle above denoting that they were minted in Mexico, and others bearing the letters 'LME' denoting that they were minted in Lima, Peru. Also, a King George II silver shilling; a King George III gold half guinea (dated 1781); thirty or so King George III gold guineas, and a Danish skilling, minted in 1771.

Glassware

Of several wine bottles, one bore the name of the vintner 'Chatfield of London'.[12] Remarkably, its cork and its contents—a red-coloured liquid— were still *in situ*. A cut-glass bowl, possibly for fruit.

Medical equipment

A vial—cylindrical vessel for containing medicines; an apothecary's cup.

Items of dress

A gold pocket watch, the inner case of which bore the name of the maker 'Jn [John] Hodges', and the place of manufacture, 'London'. The inner case is engraved with the number '1791', which at first sight suggests that the watch was made five years after *Halsewell* was lost! However, examination of its hallmark indicates a date of 1784, so it must be assumed that '1791' is the watch's serial number.[13] Needless to say, only a wealthy man could have afforded such an object. A gold winder key for a pocket watch or small clock.

A chatelaine—decorative clasp from which several chains were suspended. To these chains were attached useful household items such as keys, scissors, a watch, etc. The chatelaine recovered from *Halsewell* was made of gold, indicating that its owner was a person of high status.

A button, featuring a leaping antelope, may have been a so-called 'livery button'—the design of which related to the noble family to which the owner belonged. Many cufflinks, some in matching pairs and some single; some plain, others bearing various geometric or floral designs, the most intriguing of which was that of a balloon in flight. In the 1780s, people on both sides of the English Channel were fascinated by the concept of ballooning, the first successful manned balloon flight having taken place on 21st November 1783 when Pilatre de Rozier, the Marquess d'Arlandes, took off from the Palace of Versailles in a tethered hot-air balloon.[14] The identity of the owner of the 'balloon cufflinks' retrieved from *Halsewell* remains a mystery. Was one of her officers a ballooning enthusiast, or did the lady love of one of her young midshipmen present him with them as a gift?

Another button, the only one of its kind known to exist, is inscribed with the words 'GENERAL POST OFFICE', and with the number '107' in its centre. The G.P.O. was officially established by King Charles II in the year 1660. However, the uniform buttons of post office employees were embossed with a crown at their centre, rather than a number. *Halsewell* may well have been transporting mail (even though the Company did have its own 'packet ships', which were employed specially for the purpose). However, there is no record of any crewman aboard *Halsewell* being an employee of the G.P.O, and therefore the presence of such a button remains a mystery.

Was *Halsewell* carrying any bullion? Gold and silver bullion were in great demand in the East Indies, and in the year 1757 exports had reached a record value of £795,007.[15] Subsequently, however, limitations were placed upon such exports, and by 1780, the total value of bullion exported to India had fallen to a mere £15,041.[16] It is therefore highly unlikely that *Halsewell*'s cargo included bullion in any significant amount.

The *Halsewell* Disaster is Captured in Poetry

Down through the years, the loss of *Halsewell* in such tragic circumstances produced an outpouring of not only emotion, but also of creativity. For example, it captured the imagination of the flowing poets, among others. 'The Shipwreck of the *Halsewell* East-Indiaman: a Poem, With Very Copious and Authentic Notes, Giving a Full Account of that Very Melancholy Catastrophe, From the Sailing of the Vessel, Jan. 1st, to its Destruction, Jan. 6th, 1786'. This was the title of a poem composed in 1786, the year of the tragedy, by self-styled astronomer Evan Thomas (1733-1814) of Devizes, Wiltshire, and 'Most Respectfully Inscribed to the Honourable Directors of the East-India Company' by the author. In the preface Thomas opined (ungrammatically) that the loss of *Halsewell*

> ... was, perhaps the most naval tragical Catastrophe, that has happened for more than a Century past, and is full Proof of the Uncertainty of all transitory Enjoyments'.

Whether Captain Peirce and the officers, crew, and passengers of *Halsewell* would have regarded the prospect of a long voyage to India as a 'transitory enjoyment', bearing in mind the length of the journey and its attendant perils, is debatable to say the least.

Thomas declared that he himself 'was personally acquainted with Capt Peirce', whom he described as a man 'of distinguished Abilities, and exemplary Character'. Not only that, but 'the Character he [Thomas] has given of him, falls far short of what is due to his Merit'. As to the poem itself, it begins, dramatically, thus

OH THOU! who rulest the unfathom'd Deep,
And all its Billows in thy Hand dost keep!
Thou ridest on the Whirlwind, in thy Might!
All future Things are present in thy Sight!
Nor dare Mankind thy Providence arraign,
In Heav'n—in Earth—or on the briny Main!

With *Halsewell* in mind, Thomas now declared

'Tis not the Loss of Ships my Muse bemoans!
But *Loss of Lives*!—I hear the melting *Groans*,
Vibrating in my Ears!—One Voice I know!
'Tis Pierce's Voice—in dire Distress and Woe!
Not for himself—But for his Daughters fair,
And all the Crew, committed to his Care!

BEHOLD, alas! the awful Moment's come,
Big with the *Halsewell's* final Fate and Doom,
Inwrap'd by *Erebus**, in horrid Gloom!
She's driv'n with Fury on the much-fear'd Rock,
Splits in the Centre—Ah! I feel the Shock!

About the Captain's Neck, his Daughters cling,
As if (*poor Souls*) he could them Succour bring!
But all's in vain!—Those Shrieks and bitter Cries,
Move no Compassion in the angry Skies...

(*Erebus—'the primeval god of darkness, son of Chaos'.)[1]

Thomas followed his poem with 'A CONSOLATORY ADDRESS TO The LADY of Captain PEIRCE, And the RELATIONS and FRIENDS of all those who Lost their LIVES in the SHIPWRECK', in which he counselled the captain's bereaved widow, Mary, as follows

But hear, O Widow, be not so forlorn,
Curse not (like *Job**) the Day that you were born,
For tho' *your Bridegroom here no more you'll see*,
You'll joyful *meet him in Eternity*.
Take balmy Comfort for your Daughters too,
They've only chang'd this transient World of Woe,
For Joys unfading on th' *Elisian** Shore,
Where Storms and Tempests can disturb no more!

(*Job—a character from the *Holy Bible*. *Elysian—'relating to or characteristic of heaven or paradise'.)[2]

And Thomas concluded

> Men form vain Castles in the ambient Air,
> In search of Wealth, to distant Realms repair;
> Thoughts paint out Mines of Gold and Silver Ore,
> With glitt'ring Jewels on the *Orient* Shore!
> In search of which th' advent'rous Merchant sails,
> And spreads his Canvas, 'fore the whistling Gales;
> But God's firm Council, and his strict Decrees,
> Will ever stand, through all the Earth and Seas;
> What's best for us, He surely BEST must know;
> Under His Will let every Mortal bow!
> And without Murmur, kiss his chast'ning Rod,
> Convinc'd that He's our Father, and our GOD!

Having thus implied that Captain Peirce and his ilk were at fault for being too materialistic, Thomas advises Mary Peirce and all others who had lost relatives or loved ones in the *Halsewell* disaster, to accept uncomplainingly, perhaps even with gratitude, the fate which 'God' had ordained for them.

Henry James Pye (1745-1813), son of Admiral Thomas Pye, was Member of Parliament for Berkshire. The first verse of his descriptive poem 'On the Wreck of the *Halsewell: A Fragment*' (1787) is quoted here

> Now the loud winds with angry pinions sweep
> The laboring bosom of the stormy deep,
> The face of day o'erspread by vapors scowls,
> And 'mid the shrowds the increasing tempest howls,
> O'er the tall mast the giant surges rise,
> And a new Chaos mingles earth and skies;
> Bold even in danger's face, the naval train
> Exert their force, and try their art in vain;
> Despair and Death on all their efforts lower,
> And the loud tempest mocks their feeble power.
> Large and more large the threatening rocks appear,
> And every billow brings their fate more near.—
> Steep Purbeck's chalky cliffs, whose welcome sight
> So oft have fill'd the bosom with delight,
> When, as from hostile coasts and distant skies
> The wave-worn mariner, returning, spies

Their well-known summits with exulting eyes,
Renews each scene with thoughts domestic dear,
And wets the cheek with joy's o'er raptur'd tear,
Now in the dreadful garb of terror dress'd
Freeze life's warm tide, and chill the shuddering breast;
And the lov'd shore that life, that freedom gave,
Now sinks her sons beneath the whelming wave.

Of all the poems composed in memory of *Halsewell*, the most beautiful
and evocative was 'Lewesdon Hill' by William Crowe (1745-1829). Crowe,
cleric and theologian, was born at Midgham, Berkshire in 1745, the son of
a carpenter. He spent his childhood in Winchester, Hampshire. Having been
admitted to Winchester College as a 'poor scholar', he entered New College
Oxford, where subsequently (in 1767) he was appointed a Fellow. In 1782,
he became Rector of Stoke Abbas (or alternatively, 'Stoke Abbot') in West
Dorsetshire: a living that he held for the next five years. Crowe delivered
lectures at the Royal Institution (a London organization devoted to scientific
education and research) on poetry, and wrote several books on the subject,
including *Oratio Crewiana* (1800); *A Treatise on English Versification*,
(1827), and *Poems of William Collins, with Notes*. 'How little,' said poet,
Samuel Rogers

> ... is Crowe known, even to persons who are fond of poetry! Yet his 'Lewesdon
> Hill' is full of noble passages.[3]

Lewesdon Hill, 892 feet above sea level, is situated about a mile to the north-
west of Stoke Abbas, and this is where Crowe composed his eponymous
poem, having surmounted its summit one day in the month of May. The
poem was first published (anonymously) in 1788 by the Clarendon Press,
Oxford. One may imagine the clergyman, casting the cares of his parish
aside, for an hour or so, and entering a world where the beauty of nature,
spread out beneath him on every side, soothes his spirits and restores his
health—as the poem itself indicates.

Up to thy summit, Lewesdon, to the brow
Of yon proud rising, where the lonely thorn
Bends from the rude South-east with top cut sheer
By his keen breath, along the narrow track,
By which the scanty-pastured sheep ascend
Up to thy furze-clad summit, let me climb,—
My morning exercise,—and thence look round
Upon the variegated scene, of hills

And woods and fruitful vales, and villages
Half hid in tufted orchards, and the sea
Boundless, and studded thick with many a sail.

Ye dew-fed vapours, nightly balm, exhaled
From earth, young herbs and flowers, that in the morn
Ascend as incense to the Lord of day,
I come to breathe your odours; while they float
Yet near this surface, let me walk embathed
In your invisible perfumes, to health
So friendly, nor less grateful to the mind,
Administering sweet peace and cheerfulness.

From the vantage point of Lewesdon Hill is visible, on a clear day, the English Channel and Lyme Bay, across which *Halsewell* sailed—or to be more correct, was driven by the wind on the ultimate leg of her fateful journey. Clearly, the event, which had occurred two years previously, was very much in the mind of Crowe, as he continued with the following verses.

See how the Sun, here clouded, afar off
Pours down the golden radiance of his light
Upon the enridged sea; where the black ship
Sails on the phosphor-seeming waves. So fair,
But falsely-flattering, was yon surface calm,
When forth for India sail'd, in evil time,
That Vessel, whose disastrous fate, when told,
Fill'd every breast with horror, and each eye
With piteous tears, so cruel was the loss.
Methinks I see her, as, by the wintry storm
Shatter'd and driven along past yonder Isle,*
She strove, her latest hope, by strength or art,
To gain the port within it, or at worst
To shun that harbourless and hollow coast
From Portland eastward to the Promontory,
Where still St. Alban's high built chapel stands.
But art nor strength avail her—on she drives,
In storm and darkness to the fatal coast:
And there 'mong rocks and high-o'erhanging cliffs
Dash'd piteously, with all her precious freight
Was lost, by Neptune's wild and foamy jaws
Swallow'd up quick! The richliest-laden ship
Of spicy Ternate, or that Annual, sent

> To the Philippines o'er the Southern main
> From Acapulco, carrying massy† gold,
> Were poor to this;—freighted with hopeful Youth,
> And Beauty, and high Courage undismayed
> By mortal terrors, and paternal Love
> Strong, and unconquerable even in death—
> Alas, they perish'd all, all in one hour!

*Presumably the Isle of Portland.[4]
†'Massy'—a substantial mass of

'Lewesdon Hill' was subsequently admired by both William Wordsworth and by Samuel Taylor Coleridge.

An anonymous poem, published in 1790, is entitled 'Monody [a lament] on the Death of Captain Peirce, and those Unfortunate Young Ladies who Perished with Him, in the *Halsewell* East Indiaman'. Its first verse, however, is more reminiscent of a military campaign than of a shipwreck.

> When fierce Bellona* calls her sons from far,
> And wakes the nations with the din of war,
> Destruction o'er the peaceful valley reins,
> And tides of blood o'erflow embattl'd plains;
> Then dealing death, and crown'd with valiant deeds,
> The warlike hero for his country bleeds,

(*Bellona—Roman goddess of war.)

The poet now proceeds to describe Captain Peirce's battle with the elements.

> How long with raging winds and seas he fought,
> Suggesting all that human prudence ought!
> And when at last, of ev'ry hope bereft,
> Th'affrighted crew their sinking vessel left,
> 'Can ought be done,' he kindly ask'd, 'to save
> 'These dear Companions from the briny wave?'
> Ah hapless Parent! Who can paint thy woe!

To which the reply comes, 'They're doomed to sink, deep in the gulph below'. The poet then describes how, at the onset of the voyage, those aboard *Halsewell* were eagerly anticipating their arrival in the East Indies.

> Already to Imagination's eyes
> The glowing scenes of India's coast arise;
> Bright gems that grow beneath a warmer sun;
> And duteous slaves in countless numbers run,
> Rich palanquins, adnorn'd with fragrant flow'rs;
> And charms of wealth, and gay luxurious bowr's.

In the verses which follow, are many references to heroic characters from classical mythology, for example, Trojan warrior Hector, married to Andromache, who is killed in battle; and Aegeus, a King of Athens, who kills himself by leaping from the Acropolis! The poet now suggests how the grief of the bereaved may be assuaged

> Go search if yet in depth of Indian groves
> The virtuous Braman,* child of nature, roves;
> And, from his maxims, calmly learn to bear
> The just effects of Providence's care
> T'adore in silence all the perfect plan,
> And rev'rence what thy reason cannot scan.
> No farther yet (for sure you'll there be told)
> That all of human bliss lies not in gold,
> Nor yet in diamonds from Golconda's* mine...
>
> That to no spot of the wide earth can fin'd,
> Is found the real good of mortal kind,
> Albion†, or India, both alike possess
> The solid means of human happiness.
> That useful science these plain rules has giv'n,
> *To follow Virtue, and Submit to Heav'n.*

*Brahman—in Hinduism, the supreme universal spirit. *Golconda—diamond producing region near Hyderabad in Southern India. †Albion—Britain or England.

The theme of 'Monody' appears to be that true happiness is to be found in 'virtue', rather than in material possessions. Also, that 'providence' (or 'heaven'—which the author evidently regards as one and the same) must be 'adored' and 'revered', and what it decrees must be accepted.

Naturalist and poet Erasmus Darwin (1731-1802), spent much of his life practising as a physician in Lichfield, Staffordshire, where he established a large botanical garden. In 1791, five years after the *Halsewell* disaster, he penned the following lines, which were published in his book *The Botanic Garden*.

Oft o'er thy lovely daughters, hapless PIERCE!
    Her sighs shall breathe,
        her sorrows dew their hearse.
With brow upturn'd to Heaven, 'WE WILL NOT PART!'
He cried, and clasp'd them to his aching heart,—
Dash'd in dread conflict on the rocky grounds,
Crash the shock'd masts,
        the staggering wreck rebounds;
Through gaping seams the rushing deluge swims,
Chills their pale bosoms,
        bathes their shuddering limbs,
Climbs their white shoulders,
        buoys their streaming hair,
And the last sea-shriek bellows in the air.—
Each with loud sobs her tender sire caress'd,
And gasping strain'd him closer to her breast!—
Stretch'd on one bier they sleep beneath the brine,
And their white bones with ivory arms intwine![5]

Finally, 'The Shipwreck, or Melancholy Fate of Capt. Peirce and his Two Daughters' was composed by Elizabeth Scot (1729-1787) of Edinburgh.

Eternal Power! Who rul'st with sovereign will;
Who bid'st the tempest cease, and all is still;
In mercy hear us; stretch thine arm to save;
Oh! Snatch my children from the whelming wave.
So pray'd the parent; but the prayer was vain;
The struggling vessel sinks beneath the main.
His hapless offspring cling around their sire,
Implore his aid, and in his arms expire.
Fair, faded blossoms! ere your prime destroy'd;
To you life just was shown, and ne'er enjoy'd.
In vain bright suns and purer skies invite;
In vain is Hymen* sued to bless his rite.

*Hymen—god of marriage in Greek and Roman mythology.

A Re-enactment of the Drama: the King and Queen Pay their Respects: Charles Dickens Commemorates the Tragedy

Said Meriton, sombrely

> The misfortunes of individuals affecting only their immediate relatives, occasion no publick [*sic*] concern; and death presented in any of its ordinary forms, though at all times awful, is too familiar to be tremendous; but when numbers are involved in one common fate, and that fate is attended with circumstances of unusual horror, the united blow is felt by the whole community, the republic itself is convulsed by the shock, and grief, pity, and regret, spread themselves among all orders and conditions of men.[1]

In respect of *Halsewell*, this 'shock, grief, pity, and regret' manifested itself in various ways.

On Monday 6 March 1786, two months after *Halsewell*'s demise, *The Times* newspaper carried the following advertisement in respect of the Exeter Exchange—a London shopping mall—some of the upstairs rooms of which were let to impresarios (organizers of public entertainments), whilst others housed a menagerie ('a collection of wild animals kept in captivity for exhibition')[2]

EXHIBITION ROOMS over EXETER 'CHANGE, STRAND.

> This present MONDAY, and WEDNESDAY and FRIDAY evenings, will be presented, Mr. LOUTHERBOURGH'S EIDOPHUSIKON, Including the awful and pathetic Scene of the STORM and SHIPWRECK, conveying a very striking Idea of the late dreadful Catastrophe of the *HALSEWELL* EAST INDIAMAN.[3]

Philippe Jacques de Loutherbourg (1740-1812) was a German painter (specializing in landscapes, storms at sea, and military battles), traveller, and inventor (the eidophusikon being one of his inventions). In 1771 he had come to London, where actor, theatre manager, and playwright David Garrick, employed him as superintendent of scene painting at his theatre in Drury Lane. On 26 February 1781, De Loutherbourg

> ... in a house adjoining London's Leicester Square... opened a show described by the *Public Advertiser* as 'various imitations of Natural Phenomena, represented by moving pictures'.
>
> The show featured a glamorous specially-built theatre called an 'Eidophusikon' which seated around 130 people paying three to five shillings each. Inside, a type of giant peephole or miniature stage about 2 metres wide, 1 metre high, and 2.7 metres deep, showed five scenes of picturesque landscapes in phases of transition. Each scene ran for about three minutes, using controlled lighting, magic lantern slides, coloured silk filters, clockwork automata, three-dimensional models, painted transparencies and an accompanying sound system.

De Loutherbourg spent the remainder of his life in England, becoming a member of the Royal Academy in that same year.

In 1786, following the *Halsewell* disaster, de Loutherbourg with his eidophusikon, staged 'a simulated re-enactment' of the sinking, an event which had given rise to

> ... newspaper articles, paintings, engravings, books, pamphlets, songs and poems, as well as this first ever disaster movie and newsreel, called *The Shipwreck of the Halsewell*. Short as it was, the movie became a London sensation, and it was shown around half a century before the invention of photography.[4]

George III was born in 1738 and acceded to the throne in 1760. On 8 September 1761 he married Charlotte of Mecklenburg-Strelitz and 13 days later on 21 September, he was crowned King in Westminster Abbey. He loved the outdoor life, and took a keen interest in farming. Also, 'he took delight in models of ships and dockyards'.

In the summer of 1789, the King and Queen, and the three eldest princesses: Charlotte, Augusta, and Elizabeth, arrived at Weymouth for a 2½-month sojourn.[5] Here, they spent their time bathing, promenading, visiting the countryside, and

> ... taking trips in the frigate anchored for the purpose in the bay. In the evenings there were card parties and plays, with the King's favourite actress, Mrs [Sarah]

Siddons, to see at the theatre; and on 8 September, the [28th] anniversary of the wedding of the King and Queen, they gave a ball.[6]

There was, however, a more serious side to the visit, and it is thanks to Dorset poet William Holloway of Weymouth, that a connection between George III and the ill-fated *Halsewell* may be established, for Holloway composed the following poem, which was published in the *Western County Magazine* in October 1789.

'ON THEIR MAJESTIES AND THE PRINCESSES
VIEWING THE SPOT
WHERE THE VESSEL *HALSEWELL* WAS WRECKED'

See how, with sudden sympathy opprest,
Melts ev'ry eye, and beats each Royal breast
As you rude rocks tremendous greet the view,
And active fancy paints the scene anew—
That dreadful scene, which hapless Pierce survey'd
Thro' the dim horrors of th' incumbent shade!
Here daughters such as these, on bended knees,
Invok'd in vain that God who rules the seas;
Whilst the sad Sire appall'd—despairing stood
To hear the howling winds and dashing flood!
Struck with that thought again the salt tears flow,
And Britain's Sovereign joins the gush of woe.

Ye glorious fav'rites of an happy isle,
Whom heaven regards with an indulgent smile,
Long may you live t'adorn the sacred throne,
And weep for others' sorrows—not your own.[7]

From this it may be deduced that the King and his family visited the cliffs above the very place where *Halsewell* was shipwrecked; that the daughters knelt down in prayer; that the King, a 'family man', shed tears, undoubtedly at the immense loss of life occasioned by the tragedy, but in particular, because he empathized with Captain Peirce (two of whose own daughters had perished in the disaster).[8]

German musical composer and theorist Augustus Frederic Christopher Kollmann (1756-1829), was born in Engelbostel near Hannover, Lower Saxony. In 1782, he came to London, having been appointed organist and schoolmaster of the Royal German Chapel at St James's Palace, London.

In 1796 he composed, in memory of *Halsewell*, 'a grand instrumental piece adapted to the pianoforte, with an accompaniment for a violin and violoncello'. (There is a narrative printed both at the front of the volume and beneath the musical score, presumably to be read aloud by a narrator whilst the work was being performed.)[9]

On 31 December 1853 a short story by writer Charles Dickens (1812-1870), entitled 'The Long Voyage' appeared in *Household Words* magazine. Three dramatic maritime events are featured: namely, the so-called 'Mutiny on the Bounty' (relating to a mutiny which occurred aboard the Royal Navy vessel HMS *Bounty* in 1789 near the Tongo archipelago, in the South Pacific); the loss of the East Indiaman *Grosvenor* in August 1742, off the coast of Natal, South Africa; and the loss of *Halsewell*. On 6 April 1867 the weekly literary magazine *All The Year Round*, carried another account, by Dickens, entitled 'Old Stories Retold: The Wreck of the *Halsewell* East Indiaman'.[10]

Why was Dickens fascinated with the sea? This with it dated back to his birth in Portsmouth, Hampshire, where his father was a clerk in the Navy pay office. Furthermore, between the ages of four and eleven, he and his family lived at Chatham, Kent, also the site of a Royal Navy dockyard. It comes as no surprise, therefore, that he was fascinated by water: many of his novels featuring the sea, rivers, shipwrecks and drowning. This is particularly true of two of his lesser known novels: The *Wreck of the Golden Mary* (1856), and *A Message from the Sea* (1860).

When Dickens was aged twelve, the family relocated to Camden Town, London, which is when he was sent to work (at Warren's Blacking Factory, fixing labels to bottles of blacking—shoe polish) in order to help support his family. The factory was situated in the Strand, London, not far from Waterloo Bridge which spans the River Thames. This is, perhaps, why he began the *Wreck of the Golden Mary* with the words 'I was apprenticed to the Sea [i.e. the Thames which, being a tidal river, can loosely be referred to as the sea] when I was twelve years old…'.

In 'The Long Voyage', Dickens wrote

> When the wind is blowing and the sleet or rain is driving against the dark windows, I love to sit by the fire, thinking of what I have read in books of voyage and travel. Such books have had a strong fascination for my mind from my earliest childhood; and I wonder it should have come to pass that I never have been round the world, never have been shipwrecked, ice-environed, tomahawked, or eaten.
>
> Sitting on my ruddy hearth in the twilight of New Years Eve, I find incidents of travel rise around me from all the latitudes and longitudes of the globe. They observe no order or sequence, but appear and vanish as they will—'come like shadows, so depart'.

Dickens concluded in melancholy mood

> I stand upon a sea-shore, where the waves are years. They break and fall, and I
> may little heed them; but, with every wave the sea is rising, and I know that it
> will float me on this traveller's voyage at last.[11]

Dickens, a person capable of great emotion, would have been particularly
moved by the *Halsewell* disaster, for like Captain Peirce, he himself was a
family man, his wife Catherine having born him ten children (one of whom,
Dora Annie, had died aged only eight months).

Halsewell is Immortalized by Artists

In that year of 1786, and in the years thereafter, various artists depicted *Halsewell*, using a variety of media including watercolour, oil, aquatint*, and woodcut. (It is unlikely that any depictions of *Halsewell* were made during the ship's lifetime, and therefore these artists would have been obliged to draw their inspiration from other ships of the HEIC, built to a similar specification.)

*Aquatint—a technique of printing, involving both engraving—the inscribing of a design onto a copper plate—and the etching of this plate with nitric acid. Aquatints were used, commercially, as book illustrations and for framed prints.

The favourite themes of Robert Dodd (1748-1815), marine painter and aquatint engraver, were the French Revolutionary Wars; the American War of Independence; the River Thames; and naval dockyards. His aquatint of 1786, is entitled 'Polite Society at Sea', beneath which appear the words

> The recreation of the company on board the *Halsewell* in serene weather, three days before their disolution, on the night between the 5th & 6th of January 1786. R. Dodd fecit. Publish'd April 3 1786 by W. Dickinson No.158 New Bond Street.

In the aquatint Dodd portrays *Halsewell* as she might have looked, lying in calm waters on a bright day. In the stern gallery is Captain Peirce, in company with his two daughters, two nieces, and other female passengers, being entertained by one of the officers, who is playing the violin.[1]
'The *Halsewell* East Indiaman' by painter and illustrator of books Robert Smirke, R.A. (1752-1845), depicts Captain Peirce and his entourage on the

deck of the sinking ship, as others are borne away by the waves. The work was evidently accomplished very shortly after the loss of *Halsewell*, because only 10 weeks after the tragedy, an aquatint was made of the painting by Robert Pollard (*c.*1755-1838), painter, engraver, and publisher, and Francis Jukes (1747-1812), engraver and early specialist in aquatint, beneath the title of which appeared the words 'Painted by Robt. Smirke/ Aquatinto by F. Jukes/ Engraved by Robt. Pollard. London, Publish'd by R. Pollard Engraver No. 15 Braynes Row, Spa Fields; March 17; 1786'.

In 1787, printmaker and caricaturist James Gilray (1756-1815), using the techniques of etching, engraving, and stipple (where the surface is marked with numerous small dots or specks), created 'The Loss of the *Halsewell* Indiaman'. Based on a painting by James Northcote (Royal Academician, and pupil and biographer of Sir Joshua Reynolds), it depicts a group of men and women being tossed about by a tremendous wave, amidst broken timbers and rigging.

Thomas Stothard (1755-1834, who became a Royal Academician in 1794), specialized in illustrations for novels and works of poetry. 'The Wreck of the *Halsewell*, Indiaman, 1786' is a small oil, depicting Captain Peirce comforting his daughters in the roundhouse of the stricken ship, in company with the other ladies and the ship's officers, including Meriton and Rogers. From this painting Stothard produced a coloured mezzotint,* entitled 'Captain Peirce & Company'.

* mezzotint—a print made from an engraved copper or steel plate on which the surface has been partially roughened, for shading, and partially scraped smooth, giving light areas.[2]

England's greatest painter Joseph Mallord William Turner (1775-1851), was born on 23 April 1775, a decade before the loss of *Halsewell*, at 21 Maiden Lane, Covent Garden, London. Here, he became familiar with the Thames and with the sailing ships which plied up and down the river.[3]

Turner's 'Loss of an East Indiaman', in pencil and watercolour with additions in white chalk, was painted *c.* 1818, 32 years after *Halsewell's* demise. The painting was either commissioned by, or gifted to Walter Fawkes, landowner and Member of Parliament of Farnley Hall, North Yorkshire.

It was first exhibited by Fawkes in an exhibition held at his London home—45 Grosvenor Place—but under the (incorrect) title 'Loss of a Man of War' (which was subsequently corrected). The similarity in detail between Turner's portrayal of *Halsewell*, and the aforementioned Robert Smirke's 'The *Halsewell* East Indiaman',[4] together with the fact that Turner also mentioned the ship in one of his poems, is a strong indication that his 'Loss of an East Indiaman', is indeed a representation of the doomed *Halsewell*.

The poem referred to above was actually a fragment, which was discovered amongst Turner's papers.[5] In it, he gives a vivid description of such places as Corfe Castle, Poole and its harbour, Lulworth Cove, and St Alban's (i.e. Aldhelm's) Head—which could only have been composed by visualizing these landscapes at first hand. Furthermore, his specific mention of *Halsewell* in the poem indicates beyond doubt that he was well aware of the tragedy that had befallen her.

> Embayed the unhappy *Halsewell* toiled
> And all their efforts Neptune [?herewith] foild
> The deep rent ledges caught the trembling keel
> But memory draws the veil where pity soft does kneel...[6]

Sequel

A hatchment—large tablet, typically diamond-shaped, bearing the coat of arms of someone who has died, and displayed in their honour[1]—in memory of Captain Peirce was placed on the wall of Kingston-upon-Thames's Parish Church of All Saints.[2] The Captain's widow Mary, vacated Walnut Tree House, but, according to her last will and testament, which is dated 1807 (which is presumably when she died), she remained a resident of Kingston-upon-Thames. What of the Peirces's offspring?

Richard Peirce (junior) died in Bengal in 1795, aged 27, presumably at Calcutta, which is where his last will and testament was made. On his tombstone, located in Calcutta's South Park Street Burial Ground are written the words

> HIS MANY AMIABLE QUALITIES ENDEARED HIM
> TO SOCIETY, AND HIS FRIENDS WILL LONG
> LAMENT HIS EARLY DEATH.[3]

Thomas Burston Peirce followed in his father's footsteps, and served on the following Company ships: *Taunton Castle* (Midshipman, 1790-1); *William Pitt* (Fifth Mate, 1792-3); *Taunton Castle* (Third Mate, 1795-6); *Taunton Castle* (Second Mate, 1798-9); *Taunton Castle* (Captain, 1800-1, and 1803-4). In 1801, at Penang (named 'Prince of Wales Island' following its occupation by the Company in 1786), Malaya, Thomas married Anne Marie, daughter of Captain James Peter Fearon of the Company, by whom he had a daughter Mary Ann (born 1804). Thomas, like his elder brother, also died young. In the January–June 1863 edition of *Notes & Queries* there appeared the following entry

I may mention that the son of the Captain Peirce who was drowned, lies buried in the churchyard of Sidmouth, Devon. The grave is at twenty-five yards north of the church, for I have just measured it. The place is marked by a head and foot-stone.

This bore the inscription

In memory of Capt. T. B. Peirce, son of Capt. Peirce of the *Halsewell* E. Indiaman, obiit October 13, 1806, aged 30 years.

The date, [on the headstone] '1806' is almost illegible, but on the foot-stone it is plain. An old man, who recollects the circumstance, told me in the churchyard, that the younger Capt. Peirce, thus commemorated, died in a residence still standing, called Castle House, in the Upper High Street, Sidmouth. On the stone the name is twice [correctly] spelt Peirce, not Peirce; that is to say, the e is before the i.[4]

Emilia Peirce married William ffleming, an officer in the Company's military service; Louise Harriet Peirce married George Garrett of Portsmouth, Hampshire; Sophie Sarah Jane Peirce was married at Calcutta in 1800 to George Poyntz Ricketts, by whom she had a daughter Sophia Mary; Frances Peirce was also married at Calcutta, at the age of sixteen, to Kennard Smith, a captain and managing owner of the Company. Of the Peirce's ninth child, 'an infant' in January 1786, nothing more is known.

What became of Walnut Tree House? By the early 19th century it had become 'a very respectable school for gentlemen', known as Walnut Tree Academy and run by a Dr Harcourt. By 1841 it had ceased to be a school and 'an East India merchant' lived there 'with his wife, three children and their governess and with five female and two male servants living in'. By 1851 it was again a school; this time for young ladies. By 1861 the house had been renamed 'The Elms' and was 'the home of a retired clergyman.[5] The house was subsequently renamed (once again), 'Elmfield'.

It is known that in 1915, a Mrs Selena Walbanke-Childers was living at Elmfield. Her gardener Henry Williams Elliot, occupied the lodge at the London Road gate, and her 'jobmaster' lived in the stable block. In 1918, Elmfield was requisitioned by the War Office, but it is not known for what purpose. In 1920 the property was acquired by the local council, and Elmfield was used as a school for disabled children, with a medical clinic and dental and ophthalmic facilities. In 1929, Elmfield was acquired by Tiffin School.[6]

What of *Halsewell*'s surviving officers? In view of his previous experiences aboard the ill-fated ships *Pigot* and *Halsewell*, Second Mate Henry Meriton appeared to lead a charmed life. However, there was further drama to come, but also the chance of glory.

On 14 April 1786, only three months after the loss of *Halsewell*, Meriton set sail from Portsmouth as First Mate aboard *Bridgewater* (499 tons), bound for China, with his friend, companion, and fellow survivor from *Halsewell* John Rogers as Second Mate. Two years later, he journeyed to 'Coast & China', as First Mate aboard *Albion* (499 tons), and in 1790, he repeated the voyage aboard the same vessel. In 1792 Meriton sailed to Bombay & China, this time as First Mate aboard *Exeter*, captained by Lestock Wilson on her maiden voyage to the East. *Exeter* was one of a new generation of huge East Indiamen, which at 1,200 tons, would have dwarfed *Halsewell*. Meriton repeated the voyage twice more (in 1794 and in 1797), again in *Exeter* and again under Captain Wilson.[7]

In 1800, Meriton found himself sailing, now as captain of *Exeter*, in a flotilla of outward-bound East Indiamen, accompanied by a naval escort, the 64-gun British warship HMS *Belliqueux*. On 4 August, near the Island of Trinidade off the coast of Brazil (from whence the fleet intended to catch the westerly trade winds which would carry it to St Helena and onwards to the Cape of Good Hope), the flotilla encountered the French 40-gun frigate *Concorde*, the 36-gun frigates *Médée* and *Franchise*, and a schooner prize (enemy ship captured during the course of a naval action); the French scattered. *Belliqueux* gave chase to the *Concorde*, and Meriton's *Exeter*, together with East Indiamen *Bombay Castle*, *Coutts*, and *Neptune*, pursued the *Médée*. At 5.30 p.m., *Concorde* was captured after a brief period of resistance.[8] At 7 p.m., Meriton found himself alongside the powerful French frigate *Médée*.

> Undaunted, [he] ordered all 27 of the *Exeter*'s port gun-ports, many of them empty or unmanned, [to be] opened and bright lanterns placed behind them, lighting his ship like a fearsome, leering jack-o'-lantern ['a lantern made from a hollowed-out pumpkin or turnip in which holes are cut to represent facial features, typically made at Halloween'.[9] Then he ran alongside the *Médée* and, in stentorian tones, ordered her to surrender. The French Captain, imagining himself under the guns of a British warship, instantly complied, hauling down his flag.[10]

This was the sole occasion during the course of the French revolutionary wars (which had commenced in 1792), that a large French warship was captured by a British merchant vessel, and it was entirely due to the ingenuity of Meriton, who had succeeded in hoodwinking the enemy. However, in the course of the action, seven of *Exeter*'s ship's company had been killed in action, with another 20 wounded.

In April 1803, Meriton captained *Exeter* on a voyage to China with the so-called 'China Fleet', which on this occasion included no less than 16 East

Indiamen, commanded by Commodore Nathaniel Dance in his flagship, the *Earl Camden*. On 31 January 1804 the fleet left Canton, homeward bound with a cargo of immense value, consisting of tea, silk, and porcelain. However, there was trouble in store.

On the morning of 14 February, when the fleet was at the mouth of the Strait of Malacca (the stretch of water between the Malay Peninsula and the Indonesian island of Sumatra), four French warships were sighted. The following morning battle was joined, but in less than an hour, the French broke off the engagement.

On 14 August, the fleet arrived home to 'enormous popular acclaim', and for his part in the above action, Commodore Dance was awarded a knighthood. Also, he was presented with a sword of 100 guineas in value, and his captains each with a sword of 50 guineas in value,[11] with the name of the relevant ship engraved upon its scabbard.

*   *   *   *   *

In the year 2012, the very sword which was presented to Captain Meriton of the East Indiaman *Exeter* was sold by London auctioneers and valuers Thomas Del Mar.[12]

*   *   *   *   *

In 1807, Meriton again sailed to the East Indies as captain of *Exeter*; this time with his brother Walter Allen Meriton, as ship's purser. In March 1810, as newly appointed captain of HCS *Ceylon* (818 tons), and again with Walter as purser, Meriton set sail from Portsmouth for Madras and Bengal. However, on 3 July, off the Island of 'Mayotta' (Mayotte) in the Comoros archipelago (northern Mozambique Channel, Indian Ocean), his convoy was attacked by the French. *Astell* escaped, but *Ceylon* and *Windham* were captured and taken to the Isle de France (formerly Mauritius). Here, Meriton, his brother, and his fellow crewmen might well have remained, had the British not captured the island in December 1810 and freed them.14 By the time his seafaring career came to an end, Meriton would hold the record for having undertaken no less than thirteen voyages to the East Indies.[13]

From 1813 to 1825, Meriton served as Superintendent of the Bombay Marine, the HEIC's naval force, created to protect its merchant shipping, and to build ships for both the Company and for the Royal Navy. Meriton died on 7 August 1826, aged 64 years.

John Rogers, *Halsewell*'s Third Mate, was subsequently appointed Second Mate on *Bridgewater*, 1786-7, 1787-8; First Mate *Alfred*, 1790-1; First Mate *Ocean*, 1793-4, and 1795-6; First Mate *Exeter*, 1799-1800 (under Meriton as captain). In 1801-2 and 1802-3 he sailed as captain aboard *Admiral Aplin*, and in the same capacity aboard *General Stuart*, 1804-5, 1806-7. He finally became a managing owner.[14]

Fourth Mate Henry Pilcher, as already mentioned, did not survive, and neither did Fifth Mate William Larkins. The fate of Sixth Mate John Daniel, who did survive, is not known.[15]

On 25 October 1786 one Stephen Newman, appeared before Mr. Baron Eyre, to be tried by the second Middlesex jury. He had been indicted for

> ... burglariously and feloniously breaking and entering the dwelling house of Joseph Banfield, about the hour of seven in the night, on the 4th day of October, and burglariously stealing therein, one iron japan tea tray, value 8*s* [shillings], his [Banfield's] property.

In his defence, Newman described how, at the time in question, he was on his way to Blackwall

> to go out in the King George Indiaman; I am a gunsmith by trade, and have a wife and three children; I was going to India; I have not been able to work since I was cast away [shipwrecked] in the *Halsewell* East Indiaman.

Newman's name does not appear in Henry Meriton's list of survivors from *Halsewell* (but as already mentioned, Meriton did not claim that the list was complete), nor does he appear on the list of those soldiers who survived. Had he made up the story, in order to gain the sympathy of the court? Paradoxically, Newman was found 'guilty, but not of the burglary', and sentenced to be 'Whipped, and confined twelve months in the House of Correction'.[16]

Almost six decades later, on Wednesday 6 December 1843, it was announced in *The Times* newspaper that the previous Saturday, James Lawrence, aged 78 and 'the last of the crew of the unfortunate *Halsewell* East Indiaman', had died in Rotherhithe workhouse [a public institution in which the destitute of a parish received board and lodging in return for work[17]].[18] (Again, Lawrence's name does not appear on Meriton's list of survivors).

In yet another sequel to the *Halsewell* story, in the 10 January 1863 edition of *Notes & Queries*, the following entry appeared:

> I have a gold mourning ring enamelled, black on one side, white on the other. It has this inscription: 'Capt: R. Peirce, ae [Latin, aetatis—at the age of] 46, shipwreck'd with his dau [ghter] El [Eliza]: ae 16, & Ma [Mary]: ae 14, 6 Jan: 1786'. I believe in consequence of this catastrophe, an Admiralty Order was issued forbidding Captains of ships to have their families on board.

The author of the entry signed him or herself 'Q.D.' (unidentified).[19]

Two other mourning rings exist. The first, in the possession of Bristol Museum & Art Gallery, is described thus.

> Gold ring with horizontal octagonal glazed ivory relief within a blue enamel border: sailing ship foundering under rocky headland, masts still showing; ship's name 'HALSEWELL' inscribed on stern. On reverse, glazed compartment containing plaited hair and inscription: 'C.B.Templer//Periit Jany 6 1786'.[20]

This was the of *Halsewell*'s aforementioned midshipman, Charles Beckford Templer.

The second is the property of Captain Peirce's grandson (× 4) Richard Daglish, who describes, in his own words, how he acquired it.

> I asked in *Family Tree Magazine*, years ago, for information about *Halsewell* and Peirce and had several replies. One said that the writer had a mourning ring which a relative had bought in a junk shop, and it had the inscription:
>
> > Miss Amy Paul
> > Aged 18
> > Miss Mary Paul
> > Aged 16
> > Charles Beckford Templer, Esq.
> > Aged 15.
> > Died 6th Jany. 1786.
>
> On the outer side [face] there are strands of hair neatly wound, behind the image of a funerary urn. A few months ago I contacted the owner and agreed to buy the ring.[21]

In recent times, in a cottage in Swanage, an item of furniture—evidently the upper section of a secretaire bookcase—was discovered which bore the label, 'reclaimed from the wreck of *Halsewell*'. Its doors had originally been glazed but, understandably, the glass was missing.

A mirror, with an ornately painted wooden frame—which may have hung in one of the ship's cabins, or may have been part of a dressing table—was also washed ashore. It was evidently seen glinting in the sunshine by exciseman Barnabus Lowe of Winspit, who donated it to his niece's husband John Turner. Mrs Turner subsequently donated it to a Captain Reed, who in turn presented it to the Parish Church of St Nicholas, Worth Matravers, upon the walls of which it has hung ever since.[22]

*　　*　　*　　*　　*

In 1806, Greenland Dock, birthplace of the good ship *Halsewell*, was purchased by Greenwich timber merchant William Richie, and renamed 'Commercial Dock'. The following year Richie founded a company of the same name. Also in 1807, the rival East Country Dock Company commenced work on creating the East Country Dock (situated immediately to the south of Commercial Dock).

In 1809 another rival, the Baltic Dock Company was founded, with the objective of creating extensive 'timber ponds' (in which timbers were seasoned by being deliberately immersed in water and then dried slowly) to the north of Commercial Dock. However, in 1810, the Baltic Dock Company was acquired by Richie's Commercial Dock Company, which, in 1812, opened two new docks—Baltic and Norway.

In 1850 the Commercial Dock Company acquired the East Country Dock Company. Finally, in 1864, the Company amalgamated with the Grand Surrey Docks & Canal Company (founded in 1801 with the intention of linking Rotherhithe with Portsmouth, a project which was begun, but never completed).

Following the passing of the 1773 Regulating Act and the 1784 India Act, during the prime ministership of William Pitt, 'which established a Board of Control responsible to Parliament', the Company

> ... gradually lost independence. Its monopoly was broken in 1813, and its powers handed over to the British Crown in 1858. It ceased to exist as a legal entity in 1873.[23]

The last of the Halswell/Tynte family to own Halswell Manor was Charles John Halswell Kemeys-Tynte, 9th Baron Wharton (1908-1969), who sold the property in 1950. He died without issue, and the baronetcy passed to his sister Elisabeth Dorothy Kemeys-Tynte (1906-1974).

Epilogue

Halsewell, on her final voyage, showed herself to be a microcosm of human life, with all its virtues and with all its flaws. She epitomized hope and aspiration, endeavour and achievement, and yet at the same time the capacity of human beings to self-destruct: the ship's fate being finally sealed when her seamen made the decision to put principle before pragmatism; ideals before common sense. And by the time they realized that their failure to cooperate had been a mistake, it was too late.

The *Halsewell* experience also teaches that if it is to survive, mankind must always be on guard against the powerful and indifferent forces of nature which seek to destroy him at every turn. For nature is a promoter of entropy—the creation of what, to human minds, is disorder and randomness.

It is fitting that Dorsetshire poet William Crowe, should have the final word, and in doing so, restore a measure of calm to troubled waters.

> Yet what is music, and the blended power
> Of voice with instruments of wind and string?
> What but an empty pageant of sweet noise?
> 'Tis past: and all that it has left behind
> Is but an echo dwelling in the ear Of the toy-taken fancy, and beside,
> A void and countless hour in life's brief day.[1]

END

APPENDIX 1

Peirce Family Tree

PEIRCE FAMILY TREE

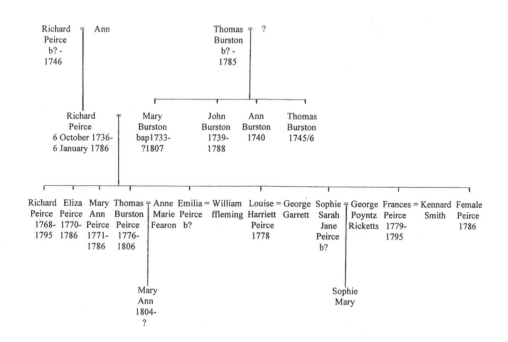

(Based on British Library, Card Index OIOC Department, and extracts from Parish Registers, Kingston-upon-Thames, Surrey)

Halsewell/Tynte Family Tree

HALSWELL/TYNTE FAMILY TREE

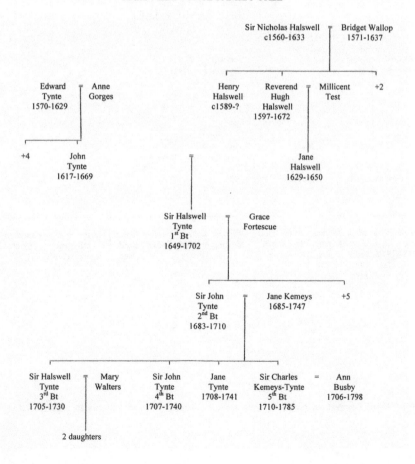

Greenland Dock and the Wells Family of Shipbuilders

In the First Edition of *A True and Particular Account of the Loss of the Halsewell* (published in 1786), which is almost entirely attributed to Henry Meriton, it is stated that the ship 'was built at Greenland-Dock, four years since'. In fact, *Halsewell* was built, not in 1782, but in 1778, by 'Wells on the River Thames'.[1] The site of Wells' shipyard at lower Rotherhithe, is clearly depicted on John Rocque's 'Plan of London, 1766'.

The story of the Wells family of shipbuilders and of how they came to acquire their shipyard, begins with Elizabeth (born *c.* 1682), daughter of John Howland and grand-daughter of Sir Josiah Child, 1st Baronet, of Wanstead, Essex; Member of Parliament for Dartmouth, Devonshire; merchant, and a governor of the HEIC.

When, in 1695, Elizabeth (evidently at the tender age of thirteen) married Wriothesley Russell, 2nd Duke of Bedford, her father, as part of her wedding dowry, gifted to her a portion of land in Lower Rotherhithe, which had originally been acquired by Elizabeth's grandfather Sir Giles Howland, Lord of Tooting Bec (who was also an early member of the HEIC). The land included a dry dock, which was leased to Abraham Wells (born *c.* 1690) of Deptford. One of a family of shipbuilders, Abraham himself was a descendant of John Wells, Paymaster of His Majesty's Navy, and owner of shipyards at Deptford. In that same year of 1695, the permission of Parliament was obtained to construct a rectangular dock at a location south of the existing dry dock. It would occupy an area of about 10 acres, and be capable of accommodating around 120 ships.

'Howland Great Wet Dock', named in honour of Elizabeth's father John, was laid out between 1695 and 1699 as a re-fitting base for ships of the HEIC. Included in the project was the construction of a new (south) dry dock, together with a north and south shipyard.

From 1725 to 1730, Howland Great Wet Dock was leased to the South Sea Company. Founded in 1711 as a joint-stock company (one whose stock is owned jointly by the shareholders), it was granted a monopoly to trade with Spain's South American colonies, under a treaty signed during the War of the Spanish Succession (1702-13). In return, the Company assumed responsibility for three fifths of national debt, which England had incurred during the course of that war. However, speculative investment caused the Company's share price to rocket, and when the 'South Sea Bubble' burst, thousands experienced financial ruin. Nevertheless, the South Sea Company continued to operate thereafter for almost three decades.

Entrepreneur Henry Elking, proposed to the governors of the South Sea Company, that they should send ships to the Arctic, in order to catch whales. (The 'Greenland Company' had been established by Act of Parliament in 1693 for this purpose, but had failed, partly on account of the disruption to maritime trade caused by wars with France.) The outcome was that 'Howland Great Wet Dock' now became known as 'Greenland Dock', and in 1725, the South Sea Company dispatched a dozen whaling ships (all built on the River Thames) to the 'Greenland Seas'. Once again, the enterprise was a failure, but nonetheless, the name 'Greenland Dock' persisted.

After Abraham Wells' death in 1755, his Deptford shipyards were sold. However, under the management of his sons John (born 1728) and William (born 1729), in partnership with banker and navy agent John Hallett, the Great Howland project expanded; the outcome being that at the Howland Great Wet Dockyard, at least one new East Indiaman vessel was launched annually.[2]

In about 1760, William Wells inherited the Holmewood Estate, Holme, Cambridgeshire from his wife's family, and thereafter the couple lived at Holmewood House. Here, their three sons: Thomas, who became a Vice Admiral in the Royal Navy; John, who became shipbuilder and banker of Blackwall Ship Yard; and William were born.

A measure of Wells Brothers & John Hallett's growing prosperity is indicated by the fact that in 1763, they purchased the Greenland Dock complex outright from its current owner John Russell, 4th Duke of Bedford. (The south yard of what was now Wells' Dock was now leased to the Burchett family who built warships for the Royal Navy).

By the mid-1770's, by which time the Wells-Hallett partnership had been dissolved, the Wells brothers continued to trade as John & William Wells. 'This partnership proved even more successful', and 'a further arrangement with East India Company Charterers resulted in the launch of 21 ships during the period 1777 to 1792'.[3] One of these was the Honourable Company Ship Halsewell.

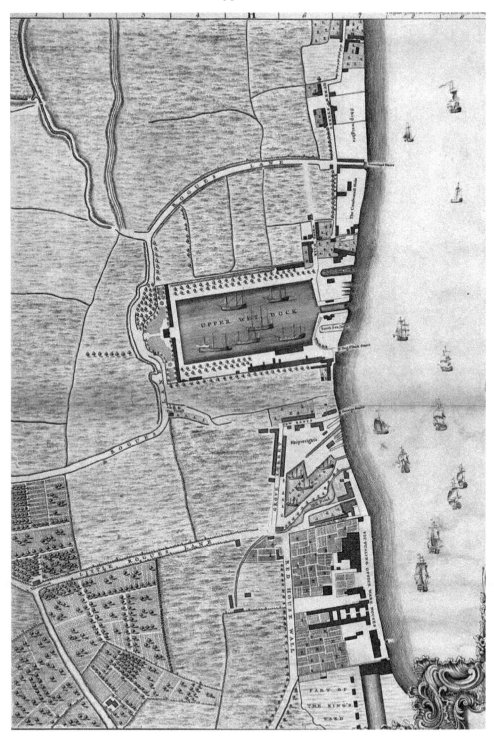

Detail from the above plan, far-right bottom panel.

A plan of London, 1746, by John Rocque, topographer to His Majesty. Howland Great
Wet Dock, later renamed Greenland Dock was originally laid out between 1695 and
1699 on land owned by the aristocratic Russell family of the 1st duke of Bedford. The
dock was intended to refit East India ships.

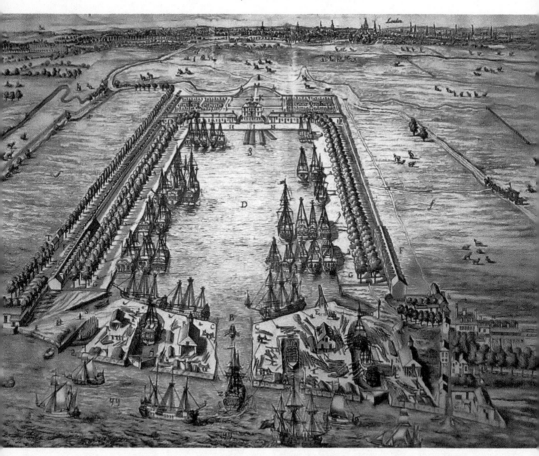

In a picture of about 1717, of Howland Great Wet Dock, it can be seen in a rural setting some miles outside the (much smaller) city of London, lined with trees on three sides to act as windbreaks.

APPENDIX 4

Uniform

Full Uniform of the Commanders and Officers in the Employ of the Honorable United East India Company.

REGULAR SHIPS.

COMMANDER.—Fine blue Coat, black Genoa Velvet round the Cuffs, four holes by two's; three outside one inside. Black Velvet Lapells, with ten holes, by two's. Black Velvet panteen Cape, with one hole on each side, straight Flaps, with 4 holes by two's. The fore Parts lined with Buff silk serge, Back slit and turns faced with the same. One Button on each hip, and one at the bottom; Gold embroidered Button Holes throughout and gilt Buttons, with the Company's Crest.

CHIEF MATE.—Blue Coat, black Velvet Lapells, Cuff and Collar with one small Button to each Cuff; Buttons to be gilt, with the Company's Crest.
SECOND MATE.—Similar Uniform to the Chief; with two small Buttons on each Cuff.
THIRD MATE.—Similar Uniform to the Chief, with three small Buttons on each Cuff.
FOURTH MATE.—Similar Uniform to the Chief; with four small Buttons on each Cuff.1

Required Qualifications for Commanders and Officers ('Mates')

QUALIFICATIONS

Of Commanders and Mates of Ships, established by the Honorable Court of Directors; 24th of January, 1804.

REGULAR SHIPS.

COMMANDER. THAT a Commander shall have attained the full age of twenty-five years, and have performed a voyage to and from India or China, in the Company's regular service, as chief or second mate, or commanded a ship in the extra service. (An 'extra ship' was one specially chartered for a particular voyage to the Far East, to provide extra cargo carrying capacity.)

CHIEF MATE. That a chief mate shall have attained the full age of twenty-three years, and have performed a voyage to and from India or China, in the Company's service, in the station of second or third mate.

SECOND MATE. That a second mate shall have attained the full age of twenty-two years, and performed a voyage to and from India or China, in the Company's service, in the station of third mate.

THIRD MATE. That a third mate shall have attained the full age of twenty-one years, and have performed two voyages to and from India or China, in the Company's service.

FOURTH MATE. That a fourth mate shall have attained the full age of twenty years, and performed one voyage to and from India or China, in the Company's service, of not less than twenty months; or one shorter voyage to and from India or China, in the Company's service, and one year in actual service in any other employ, of which last he shall produce satisfactory certificates to the Committee of Shipping.[1]

Required Inventory of Equipment etc. Necessary for Commanders and Officers

ARTICLES

The Whole, or a Selection of which, generally constitute the Investment of the Commanders and Officers, &c. of East India Ships outward.

Ale and Beer

Anchors and Grapnals

Bar Iron

Beads [i.e. of], Glass, Seed [Seed beads are uniformly shaped and spheroidal], and Ruby [Ruby beads are made from a gemstone that is a variety of the mineral corundum. Corundum of a deep, dark red colour is generally referred to as ruby. Such beads could be sold abroad for a profit]

Block Tin [i.e. ingots]

Books, Charts, &c. New Publications

Boots and Shoes

Braziery [brass cooking pans]

Bulgía Hides [presumably of Bulgarian origin]

Buntin [cloth used to make flags] of Colours

Buttons

Cabinet Ware, Desks, &c

Canvas

Cards [playing]

Carriages

Carpets

Cherry Brandy

Claret

Chronometers, Clocks, and Watches

Cloth Cuttings, Remnants, &c

Cochineal

Confectionary

Copper, Sheet, Plate, Sheathing, and Japan [a hard, dark, enamel like varnish containing asphalt, used to give a black gloss to metal objects]

Copper Nails and Fastenings

Cordage [cords or ropes, used especially in ships' rigging]

Cork

Cutlery

Cyder [cider] and Perry

Dollars [Dollar—a Spanish silver coin worth 8 reales]

Drugs

Earthen Ware

Essence of Spruce [Spruce is a coniferous tree found in the northern hemisphere. The oils from the spruce tree can be used to add a floral, citrus flavor to beer. A natural source of vitamin C, spruce essence is a prophylactic against scurvy]

Feathers, Military [presumably for attachment to a headdress to make a plume]

Furs

Glass Ware, and Window Glass of Sizes

Gunpowder, Flints, &c

Ginseng [a plant tuber credited with various tonic and medicinal properties]

Gold and Silver Lace and Thread

Haberdashery

Hardware of every Description

Hats

Hosiery

Iron, Swedish Narrow, Broad Bars, Square Bars, and Hoops

Ironmongery, Hinges, Padlocks, Locks, &c

Jewellery

Looking-glasses [mirrors]

Lines and Twines

Lead, in Pigs [ingots produced in a smelting furnace] and Sheet; Red and White

Lead Shot

Mathematical and Musical Instruments

Manchester Goods [cotton cloth made principally in Manchester, England]

Millinery

Mustard

Orsidew [or 'Dutch gold leaf', an alloy of 80% copper and 20% zinc, used to make low-priced jewellery and in thin sheets as an inexpensive imitation of gold leaf.

Oils, [Salad] and Linseed

Painters' Colours

Pitch, Tar, &c

Plate Glass

Plated Ware

Perfumery

Pickles

Pig and Sheet Lead

Port Wine

Porter, in Hogsheads and Bottles

Prints

Provisions, Salt, and of Various Kinds

Prussian Blue [a deep blue pigment used in painting and dyeing]

Quicksilver [liquid mercury]

Raisins, Bloom [currants], &c

Raspberry Brandy

Ratafia [a liqueur flavoured with almonds or the kernels of peaches, apricots, or cherries]

Rod Iron

Rum Shrub [a drink based on citrus and rum]

Saddlery of all Descriptions

Saffron

Ship's Chandlery, Lines &c

Shot, Patent, of all Sizes

Skins, China and Morocco [fine, flexible leather from Morocco], made from goatskin tanned with sumac, used especially for book covers and shoes]

Smalts [made by pulverizing blue glass and oxidizing it with cobalt to create a blue coloured pigment]

Snuff

Stationery

Steel, Bar and Faggots

Sword Blades

Tin Plates and Ware

Tobacco and Pipes

Turner's Ware [wooden bowls etc, made by turning on a lathe], Toys &c

White and Red Lead

Window and Plate Glass

Wines, Hock &c

Wooden Toys

Wrought [beaten out or shaped by hammering] Plate [a flat dish, typically made of metal]1

Required Inventory of Equipment etc. necessary for a Midshipman

NECESSARIES FOR A MIDSHIPMAN OR GUINEA-PIG,
FURNISHED BY STALKER AND WELCH,
No. 134, Leadenhall Street, London.

A Cot or Hammock

Feather Pillow

Quilts

Check Pillow-cases

White Pillow-cases

White Shirts

Black Silk Handkerchieves

Duck Trowsers [sic]

Blue Trowsers

Banyans [loose, informal gowns]

Ditto Jackets

Short Coats

Thin waistcoats with Sleeves

Calico Drawers

Sea Great-coat

Uniform Hat and Box

Dirk and Belt

Shoes

Brown Cotton Hose

Worsted [a fine, smooth yarn spun from combed long-staple wool] do.

Hair Mattrass [sic] and Bolster

Blankets

Check Sheets

White Sheets

Check Shirts

White Neck-handkerchieves

Black Silk or Velvet Stocks

Striped Trowsers

Pantaloons

Uniform Suit

Ditto Waistcoats

Lined Jackets

Flannel waistcoats with Sleeves

Flannel Drawers

Braces

Sea Hats

Leather Caps

Boots

White Cotton do.

Towels

Pocket Handkerchiefs

Foul-clothes Bag

Welch Wigs [knitted caps]

Pieces of Hair-ribbon

Sage and Balm [a fragrant ointment or preparation used to heal or soothe the skin]

Pounds of Soap

Knives and Forks

Tea Spoons

Quart Black Jack [tar]

Horn Tumblers

Set of Shoe Brushes and Blacking Cakes

Clothes Brush

Hairbrush

Sleeve Buttons

Ink-stand

Journal

Moore's Epitome2

Ephemeris [a table or data file giving the calculated positions of a celestial object at regular intervals throughout a period] or Nautical Almanac [a yearbook containing astronomical and sometimes also tidal and other information for navigators]

Gower's Treatise on Seamanship

Outline Chart, with a Scale, from England to the East Indies

Case of Instruments

Night-caps

Worsted Gloves

Needles, Thread, Tape & &c

Pieces of Shoe-ribbon

Portable Suit

Pewter Wash-hand Bason [sic]

Large Queen's Metal Spoons [Queen's metal was an alloy of nine parts tin and one part each of

antimony, lead, and bismuth. It was not then realized that lead is toxic to the system]

Pewter Plates

Pint do.

Tin Tea-kettle or Boiler

Scrubbing Brush

A Set of Combs and Brush

Small Looking-glass with Slider [It might be that on a dressing mirror or cheval mirror which has a drawer underneath it—there might be a 'slider' to facilitate reflective lighting1

Paper, Pens, Ink-powder, &c

Slate and Pencils

Bible and Prayer Book

Midshipman's Vocabulary3

Requisite Tables [Table—a set of facts or figures systematically displayed, especially in columns]

Gower's Supplement to do.

Chart of the British Channel

Gunter's Scale [Edmund Gunter (1581—1626), was an English mathematician of Welsh descent. His interest in geometry led him to develop a method of sea surveying using triangulation. Gunter's scale was a ruler, 2 feet in length and 1½ inches in breadth, and engraved on both sides, which enabled navigational calculations to be made using logarithms]

Compasses

Quadrant [an instrument used for taking angular measurements of altitude in astronomy and navigation, typically consisting of a graduated quarter circle and a sighting mechanism]

Telescope

Clasp Knives

Pen Knives

Scissars [sic]

Cork Screws

Liquor Case

Liquor

Pounds of Tobacco, in Half-Pounds

Pounds of Loaf Sugar

Pounds of Lisbon Sugar [sugar from such places as India and Brazil which was imported and refined in the Portuguese capital, and considered inferior to that imported from Jamaica and Barbados]

Sugar Cannister [Sic. Canister—a round or cylindrical container, typically one made of metal, used for storing such things as food], and Padlock

Sugar Tub and Padlock

Pounds of Green Tea in Cannisters

Pounds of Souchong [a fine black variety of China tea] in do. [Taking tea back to China, where it originated from, was something of an irony!]

Tea Pot

Butter

Cheese

Cases for do.

Log Lines [Log—an apparatus for determining the speed of a ship, originally consisting of a float attached to a knotted line wound on a reel, the distance run out in a certain time being used to estimate a vessel's speed]

Gromets [sic. Grommet—an eyelet placed in a hole in a sheet or panel to protect or insulate a rope or cable passed through it or to prevent the sheet or panel from being torn]

Clues [balls of thread]

Trunk

Chests 4

APPENDIX 8

Indulgences

THE INDULGENCE OF PRIVATE TRADE FROM THE UNITED COMPANY OF MERCHANTS OF ENGLAND TRADING TO THE EAST INDIES, To the Commanders and Officers of their Freighted Ships.

The Court of Directors of the said Company, desiring to give all due and fitting Encouragement to the Commanders and Officers of Ships employed in their Service, have resolved to allow them to participate in the Company's exclusive Trade, by permitting them to occupy Tonnage to the following Extent, in any Goods except Woollens, Camlets [woven fabrics made of camels' or goats' hair], and warlike Stores, which Articles they have thought proper to reserve, for the sole Trade and Account of the Company: and as further Indulgence to the Commanders and Officers, the Court have agreed with the Owners of Ships employed in their Service, to permit the Commanders and Officers to export and import Goods to the Extent of the Tonnage herein-mentioned,- free from any Charge for Freight.

PRIVILEGE OUTWARD.

The said Court therefore allow the Commanders and Officers of Ships in their Service, to occupy outwards the following Quantities of Tonnage, respectively, in any Sort of Goods (except as above reserved for the Trade of the Company) provided the Ship is let for 755 Tons, or upwards; and if she shall be let at a less Burthen, then they shall be allowed a less Quantity of Tonnage in Proportion, viz.

	Feet.	Tons.	Feet.
Commander		56	20
Chief Mate		8	–
Second Mate		6	–
Third Mate		3	–
Purser		3	–
Surgeon		6	–
Surgeon's Mate		3	–
Fourth Mate		2	–
Fifth Mate		1	–
Sixth Mate		–	10
Boatswain		1	–
Gunner		1	–
Carpenter		1	–
4 Midshipman, each	10	1	–
1 Ditto and Coxswain		–	10
6 Quarter-Masters, each	10	1	20
Captain's Steward		–	10
Ship's Steward		–	10
Captain's Cook		–	10
Ship's Cook		–	10
Carpenter's First Mate		–	10
Caulker		–	10
Cooper		–	10
Armourer		–	10
Sailmaker		–	10
Total Tons		96	30

[By adding the above columns, a total of 93 tons and 170 feet is arrived at, so the conclusion must be that 1 ton was equivalent to 50 (presumably cubic) feet.]

PRIVILEGE HOMEWARD

The Court also allow the Commanders and Officers of Ships in their Service, to occupy homewards the under-mentioned Quantities of Tonnage, respectively, in any Sort of Goods, subject to the Limitation in the Article of China-Ware, as hereafter-mentioned, except the Articles in the Margin.

To the Commanders and Officers of China Ships, viz.

	Tons
Commander	38
Chief Mate	8
Second Mate	6
Third Mate	3
Purser	3
Surgeon	6
Surgeon's Mate	3
Fourth Mate	2
Fifth Mate	1
Boatswain	1
Gunner	1
Carpenter	1

[The allowances for Commanders and Officers of ships other that 'China ships' were of a similar nature].[1]

APPENDIX 9

List of Wages

		£	s.	d.
1	Commander, by the Month	10	0	0
1	Chief Mate	5	0	0
1	Second Mate	4	0	0
1	Third Mate	3	10	0
1	Fourth Mate	2	10	0
1	Fifth Mate	2	5	0
1	Sixth Mate	2	5	0
1	Surgeon	5	0	0
1	Purser	2	0	0
1	Boatswain	3	10	0
1	Gunner	3	10	0
1	Master at Arms	3	0	0
1	Carpenter	4	10	0
1	Midshipman and Coxwain	2	5	0
4	Midshipman, each	2	5	0
1	Surgeon's Mate	3	10	0
1	Caulker	3	15	0
1	Cooper	3	0	0
1	Captain's Cook	3	5	0
1	Ship's Cook	2	10	0
1	Captain's Steward	2	0	0
1	Ship's Steward	2	10	0
2	Boatswain's Mates, each	2	10	0
2	Gunner's Mates, each	2	10	0
1	Carpenter's First Mate	3	5	0

1	Carpenter's Second Mate	2	10	0
1	Caulker's Mate	2	15	0
1	Cooper's Mate	2	10	0
6	Quarter-Masters, each	2	10	0
1	Sailmaker	2	10	0
1	Armourer	2	10	0
1	Butcher	2	5	0
1	Baker	2	5	0
1	Poulterer	2	5	0
2	Commander's Servants, each	1	5	0
1	Chief Mate's ditto	1	0	0
1	Second Mate's ditto	0	18	0
1	Surgeon's ditto	0	15	0
1	Boatswain's ditto	0	15	0
1	Gunner's ditto	0	15	0
1	Carpenter's ditto	0	15	0
50	Foremast Men, each	2	5	0

Total 102[1] _____

List of Officers [and crew, excluding ordinary seamen—'foremastmen'] on board the Halsewell, at the time she sailed

Richard Peirce	Captain
Thomas Burston	Chief Mate
Henry Meriton	Second Mate
John Rogers	Third Mate
Henry Pilcher	Fourth Mate
William Larkins	Fifth Mate
James Brimer	Supernumerary ditto
John Daniel	Sixth Mate
Thomas Clothier	Surgeon
Richard Fowler	Purser
" " McCoy	Surgeon's Mate
" " Falconer	Ditto
William Rayner	Purser's Assistant

Charles Templer	⌐
Charles Webber	│ Youths under the care of the Captain and
William Cowley	│ other officers, but acting as Midshipmen
[Thomas] Miller	⌐

James Welch	Gunner
Daniel Frazer	Boatswain
John Harison	Sail maker
Edward Hart	Gunner's Mate
Jacob Murray	Ditto
Thomas Barnaby	Boatswain's Mate

Benjamin Barclay	Quarter-master
James Thompson	Ditto
Andrew West	Ditto
Gilbert Ogilvie	Ditto
Joseph Jackson	Ditto
Jonath. Moreton	Ditto
Thomas Firth	Captain's Steward
George Wilson	Ship's Steward
James Jackson	Carpenter's Mate
William Fleet	Caulker's Mate
James Turner	Cooper[1]

Soldiers of the 42nd Foot, transported by *Halsewell* on her 3rd voyage List of troops for the *Halsewell* Captain Richard Peirce for Bengal

Names	Country	Occupation	Age	Height	Remarks
James Hedgcock	Kent	Labourer	19	5'-5"	Private, received onboard 29 Nov 1785
Lion. Wallis	Rutland	Labourer	18	5'-4"	Private, received onboard 29 Nov 1785
John Essea ?	Warwick	Labourer	19	5'-4"	Private, received onboard 29 Nov 1785
Edmund Barry	Cork	Labourer	22	5'-6"	Private, received onboard 29 Nov 1785
James Burnage	Worcester	Saw Maker	21	5'-8"	Received on board 19 Decs 1785 from Sick Quarters? Sulivan
William White	Hants	Labourer	24	5'-7"	Received on board 29 Nov 1785. S.Q. (Sick Quarters) 16 Dec sent out Walpole 21 Jany 86
William Pooley	Essex	Labourer	21	5'-6"	Private, received onboard 29 Nov 1785
William Japin	Middlesex	Labourer	17	5'-3"	Private, received onboard 29 Nov 1785
Mick Shais ?	Limerick	Labourer	16	5'-3"	Private, received onboard 29 Nov 1785
Alex Buckie	Scotland	Labourer	24	5'-11"	Private, received onboard 29 Nov 1785
William Johnston	Wales	Labourer	18	5'-9"	Private, received onboard 29 Nov 1785
Simon Tilly	Somerset	Cordwainer	18	5'-3"	Private, received onboard 29 Nov 1785
John Folkes or Fowkes	Middlesex	Lighterman	18	5'-5"	Private, received onboard 29 Nov 1785
Richard Reeves	Middlesex	Labourer	18	5'-5"	Private, received onboard 29 Nov 1785
William Sprag or Spaggs	Hants	Labourer	16	5'-3"	Private, received onboard 29 Nov 1785
Richard Smith	Warwick	Labourer	18	5'-3"	Private, received onboard 29 Nov 1785
John Leslie	Sunderland?	Labourer	19	5'-3"	Private, received onboard 29 Nov 1785
Robert Rickets	Devon	Labourer	16	5'-3"	Private, received onboard 29 Nov 1785

Thomas May	Devon	Labourer	16	5'-4"	Sent to Sick Quarters 24 ? sent out to the Hillsborough 8 Feby 1786
William Snow	Somerset	Labourer	22	5'-8"	Private, received onboard 29 Nov 1785
William Tranton or Trenton	Stafford	Labourer	19	5'-6"	Private, received onboard 29 Nov 1785
James Spencer	Surry	Labourer	17	5'-3"	Private, received onboard 29 Nov 1785
Edward Connor	Gloucester	Taylor [Tailor]	16	5'-4"	Received on board 29 November 1795. S.Q.(Sick Quarters) 12 Dec 1785 sent to Valentine 8 Jany 86??(S 2 may be 'Sick Quarters'?)
Joseph Murray	America	Cordwainer	18	5'-3"	Private, received onboard 29 Nov 1785
Thomas Lock	Kent	Labourer	21	5'-7"	Private, received onboard 29 Nov 1785
Robert Caineson	Edinburgh	Labourer	26	5'-8"	Private, received onboard 29 Nov 1785
John Downes	Ireland	Labourer	19	5'-4"	Private, received onboard 29 Nov 1785
? Jacob	Kent	Labourer	31	5'-6"	Private, received onboard 29 Nov 1785
Jacob Cooper	Middlesex	Labourer	20	5'-6"	Private, received onboard 29 Nov 1785
Janus Wade	Suffork	Labourer	17	5'-3"	Private, received onboard 29 Nov 1785
Micheal Murphy	Ireland	Cardmaker?	19	5'-6"	Private, received onboard 29 Nov 1785
John Howse	Norfolk	Labourer	19	5'-4"	Private, received onboard 29 Nov 1785
James Durant	Suffolk	Labourer	21	5'-7"	Private, received onboard 29 Nov 1785
Richard Clifton	Lincoln	Labourer	19	5'-6"	Private, received onboard 29 Nov 1785
Thomas Jackson	Cambridge	Labourer	19	5'-5"	Private, received onboard 29 Nov 1785
Thomas Harman	Dublin	Taylor	24	5'-7"	Private, received onboard 29 Nov 1785
William Easton	Middlesex	Labourer	16	5'-3"	Private, received onboard 29 Nov 1785
John Meason	Cornwall	Labourer	19	5'-8"	Private, received onboard 29 Nov 1785
William Rigge	Middlesex	Labourer	18	5'-3"	Private, received onboard 29 Nov 1785
Samuel Masnigaib ?	Cambridge	Labourer	16	5'-3"	Private, received onboard 29 Nov 1785
William Carter	Lancashire	Labourer	22	5'-6"	Private, received onboard 29 Nov 1785
Henry Townsend	Berks	Labourer	30	5'-8"	Private, received onboard 29 Nov 1785
William Baker	Herts	Labourer	25	5'-10"	Private, received onboard 29 Nov 1785
John Wyatt	Devon	Presser?	16	5'-3"	Private, received onboard 29 Nov 1785
John Sizemon	Worcester	Baker	18	5'-4"	Private, received onboard 29 Nov 1785
John Watts	Sheffield	Labourer	30	5'-7"	Run 29 Dec 1785 (i.e. deserted)
James Rowley	Lye	Labourer	29	5'-8"	Private, received onboard 1 Dec 1785
James Johnson	America	Labourer	26	5'-7"	Private, received onboard 1 Dec 1785
John Cox	Hants	Labourer	17	5'-4"	Private, received onboard 1 Dec 1785
Thomas Jones	Lincoln	Labourer	23	5'-8"	Private, received onboard 1 Dec 1785
John Jones	Herts	Labourer	19	5'-4"	Received on board 1st December 1795. Sent to S.Q (Sick Quarters) 13 Dec? sent on Phoenix 9 Jany? removed? to the Walpole 10 Jany
Caleb Austin	American	Labourer	21	5'-11"	Private, received onboard 1 Dec 1785

John Dawson	Cumberland	Labourer	30	5'-10"	Private, received onboard 1 Dec 1785
Edward Ellery ?	Hants	Labourer	17	5'-3"	Private, received onboard 1 Dec 1785
John Dunn	Middlesex	Labourer	18	5'-4"	Private, received onboard 1 Dec 1785
John Todd	York	Labourer	18	5'-5"	Private, received onboard 1 Dec 1785
Joseph King	Hants	Labourer	18	5'-4"	Received on board 1st December 1795. Run 29 Dec 1785 (i.e. deserted)
James Gorman	Ireland	Labourer	17	5'-5"	Private, received onboard 1 Dec 1785
Watkin Morris	Middlesex	Labourer	16	5'-4"	Private, received onboard 1 Dec 1785
Henry Shafton	Essex?	Sawyer?	22	5'-6"	Private, received onboard 1 Dec 1785
John Witford	Worcester	Labourer	16	5'-3"	Private, received onboard 1 Dec 1785
Thomas Herriman	York	Taylor	19	5'-5"	Private, received onboard 1 Dec 1785
James Andrews?	Worcester	Labourer	18	5'-3"	Private, received onboard 1 Dec 1785
George Haynes	Middlesex	Labourer	16	5'-3"	Private, received onboard 1 Dec 1785
James Douglas	Edinburgh	Labourer	17	5'-6"	Private, received onboard 1 Dec 1785
Thomas Saunders	London	Weaver	20	5'-7"	Private, received onboard 1 Dec 1785
John Sinddall ?	Cambridge	Labourer	22	5'-11"	Private, received onboard 1 Dec 1785
Mathew Mahoney	Ireland	Labourer	26	5'-7"	Private, received onboard 1 Dec 1785
Robert Daniel	Middlesex	Blacksmith	22	5'-7"	Private, received onboard 1 Dec 1785
Thomas Ruffeler	Surry [Surrey]	Labourer	18	5'-4"	Received on board 1st December 1795. S.Q (Sick Quarters) 22 Dec sent out Phoenix 9 Jany removed to the Walpole 20 Jany?
John Sturley ?	Norfolk	Butcher	18	5'-5"	Private, received onboard 1 Dec 1785
John Kirby	Herts	Labourer	25	5'-9"	Private, received onboard 1 Dec 1785
Thomas Eastman	Wilts	Labourer	20	5'-6"	Private, received onboard 1 Dec 1785
Thomas Arnold?	America	Labourer	19	5'-6"	Received on board 1st December 1795. Run 29 Dec 1785 (i.e. deserted)
Thomas Asley ?	Dublin	Pinmaker?	19	5'-3"	Private, received onboard 1 Dec 1785
John Black	Middlesex	Bucklemaker	19	5'-5"	Received on board 1st December 1795. Discharged 1 Dec 1785
John Williams	Lanarkshire?	Labourer	18	5'-3"	Received on board 1st December 1795. S.Q (Sick Quarters) 22 Decr sent out Hillsborough 3 Feby?
William Black	Ireland	Weaver	24	5'-6"	Private, received onboard 1 Dec 1785
James Shields or Shield	Down?	Labourer	19	5'-4"	Private, received onboard 1 Dec 1785
John Angel	Herts	Labourer	16	5'-5"	Received on board 1st December 1795. S.Q? (Sick Quarters) 22 Dec sent out Pheonix 9 Jany removed to the Walpole the 10 Jany
Iain ? Woodcock	Gloucester	Labourer	30	5'-8"	Private, received onboard 1 Dec 1785
Joseph Thomas	Middlesex	Labourer	27	5'-6"	Private, received onboard 1 Dec 1785

George Hancock	Hants	Taylor	27	5'-7"	Private, received onboard 1 Dec 1785
Thomas White	Ireland	Labourer	30	5'-8"	Private, received onboard 1 Dec 1785
Andrew Johnson	Scotland	Labourer	19	5'-5"	Private, received onboard 1 Dec 1785
Richard Stovell or Strover	Surry	Labourer	26	5'-6"	Private, received onboard 1 Dec 1785
John Streeter ?	Middlesex	Bricklayer	24	5'-10"	Private, received onboard 1 Dec 1785
? Mathews	Ireland	Hairdresser?	19	5'-5"	Private, received onboard 1 Dec 1785
Joseph Watson	Kent	Labourer	19	5'-3"	Private, received onboard 1 Dec 1785
Pat Giraghty or Ganetty	Ireland	Labourer	20	5'-6"	Private, received onboard 1 Dec 1785
William Varnell	Herts	Labourer	28	5'-6"	Private, received onboard 1 Dec 1785
James Thompson	Northumberland	Taylor	32	5'-6"	Private, received onboard 1 Dec 1785
Joshua Hawkins	Middlesex	Labourer	18	5'-5"	Private, received onboard 1 Dec 1785
Moses Langford	Sussex	Labourer	16	5'-3"	Private, received onboard 1 Dec 1785
Benjamin Morris	Herts	Labourer	19	5'-4"	Private, received onboard 1 Dec 1785
Joseph Allen	Bucks	Labourer	18	5'-6"	Private, received onboard 1 Dec 1785
Pat Ryan	Dublin	Corporal	26	5'-5"	Captain of Infantry, received onboard 3 Dec 1785. Applied 25 Nov. pd £4.10 & 13/8???
Thomas Perryman	Somerset	Sergeant	31	5'-5"	Sergeant of Infantry, received onboard 17 Dec 1785. pd £4.10 &13/8 in lieu Bed???
Philip Smith	London	Labourer	18	5'-3"	Private, received onboard 1 Dec 1785
Richard Barnes	Dorking, Surry	Hatter?	19	5'-5"	Private, received onboard 1 Dec 1785
William Pink	Lincoln	Labourer	17	5'-3"	Received on board 29 Nov. Run 29 Dec. 1785 (i.e. deserted)
John Wilkinson	Herts	Labourer	18	5'-5"	Private, received onboard 19 Dec 1785 from S.Q. (Sick Quarters) Sulivan?
David Laidlor	Twedale	Soldier	27	5'-10"	Matross, received onboard 12 Dec 1785. paid in lieu ?? of Bed £2.5.6

The Three Voyages of HCS *Halsewell*

First Voyage: 1778-81
Halsewell
758 Tons, 1 Voyage
COAST AND CHINA

(Thomas Burston, Esq.)
Capt. Richard Peirce
1 John Eastabrooke
2 Joseph Garnault
3 Thomas Burston
4 John Stewart
Sur. [Surgeon] James Gent
Pur. [Purser] William Graham
Sailed Ports. [Portsmouth, Hampshire] 7 March, 1779*
Arr. [Arrived] Downs 20 Oct. 1781[1]
*NB, *Halsewell* sailed from Gravesend on Tuesday 1 December 1778.[2]

Second Voyage: 1782-4
Halsewell
758 Tons, 2 Voyage
COAST AND BAY.

(Thomas Burston, Esq.)
Capt. Richard Peirce
1 Thomas Burston
2 Ninian Lewis
3 Thomas Smith
4 Martyn Chamberlayne

Sur. Charles Bromfield
Pur. Richard Fowler
Sailed Ports. 11 March, 1783*
Arr. Downs 28 Aug. 1784[3]

*NB, *Halsewell* departed from Gravesend on 24 December 1782.[4]

Third Voyage: 1786-
Halsewell
758 Tons, 3 Voyage
COAST AND BAY

(Peter Esdaile, Esq.)
Capt. Richard Peirce
1 Thomas Burston
2 Henry Meriton
3 John Rogers
Sur. Thomas Clothier
Pur. Richard Fowler
Sailed Downs 1 Jan. 17865

Halsewell's Logbook: an Explanation

For a given day, column 1, headed 'H', contained the numbers 1-12 (representing 1 p.m. to 12 midnight) followed by 1-12 again (representing 12 midnight to 1 p.m.). The second column was for the course, steered by magnetic compass and recorded on an hourly basis. The third and fourth columns, headed 'K' and 'F', were for the vessel's speed in knots and fractions of knots. The fifth column contained a note of the wind's direction and strength, and the general weather conditions. Finally, in the sixth column were included any remarks concerning the general management of the ship, together with additional information such as barometric pressure.

In the bottom row, beneath the heading 'Course' was recorded the direction followed over the previous 24 hours; beneath 'D' the distance travelled; beneath (say) 'S' (southings) the distance travelled southwards, and beneath, say 'E' (eastings), the distance travelled eastwards; beneath 'MD' (meridian + distance) the distance east or west of the zero meridian from which the vessel took its last departure; 'X Lo indicated the difference in longitude from the previous day's position; 'Lo in' states the longitude according to the Greenwich meridian, and finally 'Bearing & Distance' related to where the ship was, in relation to its starting point.

Ships' Stores

PARTICULARS OF STORES, OUTWARD, Allowed the undermentioned Officers of REGULAR SHIPS AS INDULGENCE

Chief Mate	24	Dozen of Wine, or Beer.
	2	Firkins [firkin—a cask of about 12 gallons in capacity] Butter.
	1	Cwt. Cheese
	1	Ditto Grocery.
	4	Quarter Cases Pickles.
Second Mate	20	Dozen of Wine or Beer, the other Articles, the same as Chief Mate.
Third Mate	16	Dozen of Wine or Beer.
For the Mess	6	Hogsheads Beer.
	7	Firkins Butter.
	3	Cwt. and a Half Cheese.
	2	Cwt. Grocery.
	16	Quarter Cases Pickles.
	20	Hams.
*Fourth Mate	12	Dozen of Wine or Beer.
*Fifth Mate	10	Dozen of Wine or Beer.
Surgeon	14	Dozen of Wine or Beer, the other Articles, the same as Chief Mate.
*Surgeon's Mate	12	Dozen of Wine or Beer.
Pursers	16	Dozen of Wine or Beer.
	2	Firkins Butter.
	1	Cwt. Cheese.
	½	Ditto. Grocery.
	4	Quarter Cases Pickles.

*The Fourth Mate is allowed—2 Firkins Butter, 1 Cwt. Cheese. ½ ditto. Grocery, 1 Case Pickles.—Also the Fifth and Surgeon's Mates each—1 Firkin Butter, ½ Cwt. Cheese, ½ ditto. Grocery, 1 Case Pickles, but it is given to the Third Mate for the Mess.

Boatswains, Gunner's,	10	Dozen of Wine or Beer.
and Carpenter's	1	Firkin Butter.
Stores, each.	½	Cwt. Cheese.
	½	do. Grocery.
	4	Quarter Cases Pickles.

And on Petition are further allowed as under:

	½	do. Grocery.
	4	Quarter Cases Pickles.
	1	Punchion Spirits for the Mess of the Chief, Second Mate, Surgeon, and Purser
	1	Punchion Spirits for the Mess of the Third Mate[1]

APPENDIX 15

List of Officers, Seamen, and Soldiers saved

Henry Meriton	Second Mate
John Rogers	Third Mate
John Daniel	Sixth Mate
Duncan McDougal	Midshipman
—— McManus	Ditto
James Welch	Gunner
Daniel Frazer	Boatswain
John Harrison	Sail-maker
Jacob Murray	Ditto
Thomas Barnaby	Boatswain's Mate
Benjamin Barclay	Quarter-master
James Thompson	Ditto
Andrew West	Ditto
Gilbert Ogilvie	Ditto
Joseph Jackson	Ditto
James Jackson	Carpenter's Mate
WilliamFleet	Caulker's Mate
James Turner	Cooper
Robert Pierce	Cook
Richard Tupman	Seaman
Thomas Morgan	Ditto
John Lock	Ditto
Timothy Forster	Ditto
George Woodgate	Ditto
Andrew Anderson	Ditto
John Morris	Ditto

George Harris	Ditto
Wm. Viccary	Ditto
John Cownden	Ditto
Robert Millar	Ditto
David Anstey	Ditto
William Thompson	Ditto
George Sunderland	Ditto
Jonath. Rogers	Ditto
Nath. Mingies	Seaman
John Price	Ditto
John Love	Ditto
Thomas Brooks	Ditto
Solomon Bevans	Ditto
Michael Bevans	Ditto
Robert Humphries	Ditto
Richard Berry	Ditto
John White	Ditto
Peter Ross	Ditto
Thomas White	Ditto
John Anderson	Ditto
George Ruffell	Ditto
Robert Roberts	Ditto
William Evans	Ditto
James Flendall	Ditto
George Powdrill	Ditto
John Fowles	Soldier
Joshua Hawkins	Ditto
William Gapon	Ditto
James Rowley	Ditto
Richard Strover	Ditto
Thomas Jones	Ditto
Robert Daniel	Ditto
William Spraggs	Ditto
Thomas Eastman	Ditto
William Clark	Ditto
William Rickies	Ditto
John Morse	Ditto
Caleb Austen	Ditto
Joseph Watson	Ditto
Thomas Shaftoe	Ditto
John Todd	Ditto
William Johnston	Ditto

Richard Reeves	Ditto
Philip Smith	Ditto
Patrick Ganetty	Soldier
Benjamin Morris	Ditto
Thomas Sanders	Ditto
James Shield	Ditto
John White	Ditto
William Trenton	Ditto

[From this, it appears that the number of seamen saved was 33, and the number of soldiers saved was 25.][1]

The History of Walnut Tree House

Captain Richard Peirce was the most recent of a long line of distinguished occupants of the house. Originally, it had probably been a gentleman's residence from at any rate the 1680's, but it had once been a farm, called the Chapel Farm because it had belonged to the neighbouring Lovekyn Chantry Chapel... [named after Edward Lovekyn, a Kingston caterer (1239-1310) and founded as a Chantry Chapel—endowed for a priest or priests to celebrate masses for the soul of its founder—in 1309].

In 1738 the house was bought by a London gentleman with the splendidly eighteenth century name of Peregrine Fury, Esq. The property was then described as a Capital messuage [principal dwelling house with outbuildings and land assigned to its use], barns, stables, coach houses, dovehouse, room and granary under the dovehouse, outhouses, etc., with nine acres of land adjoining and also the farmyard lately converted into a garden.... There was also a pew [i.e. reserved for the owner of the house] in Kingston Church.

Walnut Tree House was often let, usually for short terms to wealthy tenants. In 1747/48, for example, it was occupied by Admiral [William] Martin.... Soon after, the tenant was Lady Selina Bathurst, the recently widowed daughter of Earl Ferrers. She was succeeded [as a tenant] by the wealthy Robert Linch Bloss, heir to an Irish Baronetcy.

In the early Georgian period, it became fashionable to think red brick too glaring and [instead] to use yellow stock bricks [hand made in traditional brickworks] for new houses.

This was the type of brick used by Mr. Fury when he rebuilt Walnut Tree House in 1756-7, and presumably laid out the gardens and 'fashionable lawns' at the same time. Fury 'died in 1759, after which time the property remained in the hands of his family until 1825'.

Mr Fury's son, also Peregrine... lived in the new house until 1773, but also had a town house in London's Grosvesnor Street. After this the house was [again] let and in 1775/76 the tenant was another newly-married man, the Fourth Duke of Atholl, then only twenty years old.[1]

Endnotes

Preface

1 It was not until 1 January 1801 that Great Britain and Ireland became unified, after which George III became King of the United Kingdom of Great Britain and Ireland.
2 Oxford Dictionaries Online

Chapter 1

1 *Hist. MSS. Comm. Salisbury*, x, pp.445-6 (1600), in Lipson, Ephraim, *Economic History of England*, Volume 2, p. 271.
2 Bowman, Florence L., and Esther G. Roper, *Traders in East and West*, p. 36.
3 *The First Letter Book of the East India Company*, p. 429; State Papers East Indies, 1513-1616, pp. 231-2, in Lipson, Ephraim, *Economic History of England*, Volume 2, pp. 275-6.
4 Lipson, *op. cit.*, Volume 2, pp. 275-6.
5 Rawlinson, H. G., *British Beginnings in Western India, 1579-1657: An Account of the Early Days of the British Factory of Surat*, pp. 47-8, from original manuscripts in the India Office in the *Lancaster Voyages*, edited by Albert H. Markham for the Hakluyt Society.
6 Lipson, Ephraim, *op. cit.*, p. 291.
7 Information kindly supplied by the Seadart Divers Association.
8 Information kindly supplied by the Department of Coins and Medals, Fitzwilliam Museum, Cambridge.
9 Information kindly supplied by the Seadart Divers Association.

Chapter 2

1　'An owner who had been accustomed to charter one of his ships to the Company had a proprietary right to supply other ships when this one had been worn out'. Chatterton, E. Keble, *A World for the Taking: The Ships of the Honourable East India Company*, p. 117. (However, this right appears to have been waived in respect of the *Earl of Ashburnham*, whose owner was John Durand.)

2　Matthew, H. C. G., and Brian Harrison (Editors) *Oxford Dictionary of National Biography*.

3　Larn, Richard and Bridget, *Shipwreck Index of the British Isles*, Volume I, Section 6.

4　Meriton, Henry, *A True and Particular Account of the Loss of the Halsewell*, p. 4. N.B. Because of the similarities between *A Circumstantial Narrative of the Loss of the Halsewell*, which is definitely attributed to Henry Meriton (and John Rogers), and *A True and Particular Account of the Loss of the Halsewell*, (both published in 1786), the latter volume is also assumed to have been written by Meriton.

5　Oxford Dictionaries Online.

6　The larger cables were made of hemp—the fibre of the cannabis plant, extracted from the stem—and the smaller from coir—the external fibres of the coconut, which grew in abundance in India. Chatterton, E. Keble, *op. cit.*, p. 115.

7　Hardy, Charles and Horatio Charles Hardy, *A Register of Ships, Employed in the Service of the Honorable the United East India Company, from the year 1760 to 1810*, pp. 55-7.

8　Chatterton, E. Keble, *op. cit.*, pp.152-3.

9　Oxford Dictionaries Online. Scurvy is now known to result from a deficiency of Vitamin C in the diet.

10　Chatterton, E. Keble, *op. cit.*, p. 172.

11　*Ibid.*, p. 174.

12　*Ibid.*, p. 153.

13　Oxford Dictionaries Online.

14　Chatterton, E. Keble, *op. cit.*, p. 152.

15　British Library, *Halsewell Journal*, L/MAR/B/465C.

16　 Miller, Russell, *The East Indiamen*, p. 171.

17　Miller, David, *The World of Jack Aubrey*, pp. 90, 87.

18　Oxford Dictionaries Online.

19　Miller, Russell, *op. cit.*, p. 130. In 1799, regulations were drafted to this effect.

20　Chatterton, E. Keble, *The Old East Indiamen*, p. 249

21　Chatterton, E. Keble, *A World for the Taking: The Ships of the Honourable East India Company*, pp. 172-3.

22　From Lady Anne Barnard's account of a voyage in the East Indiaman *Sir Edward Hughes* in 1797, in Russell Miller, *op. cit.*, p. 129.

23　Brough, Anthony, *Considerations on the Necessity of Lowering the Exorbitant Freight of Ships employed in the Service of the East-India Company*, p. 34.

24 The elaborate 'engine', by which the ship's wheel worked the tiller—the horizontal bar fitted to the head of the rudder and used for steering—was invented by a 'Mr Pollard', Master Shipwright at the Royal Naval Dockyard, Portsmouth. The gentleman referred to was probably Thomas Pollard, who served in the same capacity at Sheerness (1782-4), Devonport (1784-93), Chatham (1793-4), and Deptford (from 1795.) Attached to the tiller were ropes, which were led by a system of 'sweeps [a 'sweep' being a piece of timber in the shape of an arc, used to support the end of the tiller] and rowles' [a rowle being the pivot of a whipstaff—the vertical lever at the end of the tiller] to the ship's wheel, which was mounted on the quarterdeck.

Chapter 3

1 Bowman, Florence L., and Esther G. Roper, *Traders in East and West*, p. 36.
2 Oxford Dictionaries Online.
3 Bowman, Florence L., and Esther G. Roper, *op. cit.*, pp. 37-8.
4 Chatterton, E. Keble, *A World for the Taking: The Ships of the Honourable East India Company*, p. 119.
5 'An Exact Description of the Growth, Quality and Virtues of the Leaf Tea, by Thomas Garway in Exchange Alley, near the Royal Exchange in London' [1660?], in Bowman, Florence L., and Esther G. Roper, *op. cit.*, pp. 46-7.
6 'Chinese Rarities brought on an East India Ship, May 22, 1664', The *Diary of John Evelyn*, London, 1906, volume II, p. 210, in Bowman, Florence L., and Esther G. Roper, *op. cit.*, pp. 50-1.
7 'Cargo of India Ship, November 16, *1665*', *Diary of Samuel Pepys*, London, 1906, p. 360, in Bowman, Florence L., and Esther G. Roper, *Traders in East and West*, p. 50.
8 Bowman, Florence L., and Esther G. Roper, *op. cit.*, pp. 39-41.
9 Spencer, Alfred (Editor), *Memoirs of William Hickey*, Volume 4, p. 245.

Chapter 4

1 British Library, Asia, Pacific and Africa Collections, N/1/1, folio 194.
2 Richard Peirce, baptized on 6 October 1736, Calcutta.
3 Marriage of 'Richard Peirce [here on the marriage certificate, the surname is spelt correctly], Batchelor', to 'Mary Burston, Spinster', 25 September 1767, Certificate No. 199. Like her husband, Mary was also born at Calcutta. The name 'Richard Peirce' appears on the marriage certificate as a witness. However, as Richard Peirce senior is believed to have been buried in Calcutta on 14 September 1746 (information kindly supplied by Richard Daglish), this Richard was presumably another member of the family whose identity is unknown. Although Thomas Burston Esquire is listed only as managing owner of HCS *Halsewell*, he may have had a lesser shares in other vessels.

4 Captain Peirce and his wife Mary's offspring were Richard (junior, born 1768); Eliza (born 1770); Mary Ann (born 1771); Thomas Burston (born 1775 or 1776); Emilia (born ?); Louise Harriet (1778); Sophie Sarah Jane (born ?); Frances (born 1779),4 and an unidentified daughter, born in late 1785, who is believed not to have survived to adulthood). From Parish Registers, Kingston-upon-Thames, Surrey.

5 Meriton, Henry, *A True and Particular Account of the Loss of the Halsewell*, p. 4.

6 The meaning of this word is not known.

7 Hardy, Charles and Horatio Charles Hardy, *A Register of Ships, Employed in the Service of the Honorable the United East India Company, from the year 1760 to 1810*, p. 111.

8 Information kindly supplied by National Army Museum, London.

9 Miller, Russell, *The East Indiamen*, p. 122.

10 *Ibid.*, p. 129.

11 A full list of wages paid to the various members of a ship's company appears in Appendix 7.

12 Hardy, Charles and Horatio Charles Hardy, *op. cit.*, p. 67. Although these figures are for the year 1810, it is likely that those which obtained in 1786 were of a similar nature.

13 *Ibid.*, p. 63.

14 Sutton, Jean, *Lords of the East: The East India Company and its Ships*, p. 73.

15 *Ibid.*, p. 74.

16 Cotton, Sir Evan, *East Indiamen*, p. 37.

Chapter 5

1 Captain Shane's Company of his Majesty's 73rd (Highland) Regiment of Foot (MacLeod's Highlanders).

2 Oxford Dictionaries Online.

3 British Library, *Halsewell Journal*, L/MAR/B/465A-B.

4 Oxford Dictionaries Online.

5 *Ibid.*

6 Information kindly supplied by Wally Hammond.

7 Possibly Edward Dampier, formerly a captain in the Company's service, and now one of its officials.

8 British Library, *Halsewell Journal*, L/MAR/B/465A-B.

Chapter 6

1 Meriton, Henry, *A True and Particular Account of the Loss of the Halsewell*, pp. 21-2.

2 Matthew, H. C. G., and Brian Harrison (Editors) *Oxford Dictionary of National Biography*.

3 British Library, *Halsewell Journal*, L/MAR/B/465C.

Chapter 7

1 Meriton, Henry, *A True and Particular Account of the Loss of the Halsewell*, p. 4.

2 Hardy, Charles and Horatio Charles Hardy, *A Register of Ships, Employed in the Service of the Honorable the United East India Company, from the year 1760 to 1810*, p. 179.

3 *Ibid.*, p. 111.

4 Meriton, Henry and John Rogers, A Circumstantial Narrative of the Loss of the Halsewell, pp. 64-5.

5 Hardy, Charles and Horatio Charles Hardy, *op. cit. Pigot* appears to have been an unlucky ship, for on 9 February 1794, captained by George Ballantyne, she was captured by the French in the Sunda Strait, Indonesia.

6 Meriton, Henry and John Rogers, *op. cit.*, pp. 71-2, and *The Times*, 10 January 1786.

7 Information kindly supplied by Mrs Valerie Allen, widow of the late David John Allen.

8 Miller, Russell, *The East Indiamen*, p. 122.

9 *Ibid.*, p. 123.

10 In 1659, the English acquired the South Atlantic island of St Helena as a port of call for homeward-bound ships. It was lost to the Dutch in 1672, but retaken by the English in the following year. It was appropriate for British merchant ships to fly the Red Ensign. However, beyond St Helena, and in eastern waters, they were also permitted to fly the flag of the Company.

11 Hardy, Charles and Horatio Charles Hardy, *op. cit.*, p. 113.

12 Meriton, Henry and John Rogers, *op. cit.*, pp. 56-7.

13 The age given on his tombstone in Christchurch Priory.

14 Meriton, Henry and John Rogers, *op. cit.*, pp. 72-3.

15 http://en.wikipedia.org/wiki/Midshipman14

16 Partridge, Eric, *A Dictionary of Slang and Unconventional English*.

17 Oxford Dictionaries Online.

18 Meriton, Henry and John Rogers, *op. cit.*, p. 72.

19 See Appendix 7.

20 Meriton, Henry, *op. cit.*, p. 4.

21 *Hampshire Chronicle*, after 14 January 1786, and Cotton, Sir Evan, *East Indiamen*, p. 128.

22 Information discovered by Ed Cumming & James Derriman in the British Library archives, Reference BL-OIOC, and L/MIL//9/91, see Appendix 9.

23 The fact that these senior ranks were present may be inferred from an undated letter subsequently sent by M. Lewis Esq., of the War Office... requesting Thomas Morton to move the Court of Directors to provide room on one of the Company's ships bound for Bengal for clothing for the 2nd Battalion 42nd Regiment replacing that lost on the *Halsewell*, and for passages for a Captain and four ensigns of the 2nd Battalion.

24 Meriton, Henry, *op. cit.*, p. 4.

25 Miller, Russell, *op. cit.*, p. 122.

26 Spencer, Alfred (Editor), *Memoirs of William Hickey*, Volume 1, p. 121.

27 Meriton, Henry, *op. cit.*, pp. 4-5.

28 *Hampshire Chronicle*, Monday 16 January 1786.

29 Meriton, Henry and John Rogers, *op. cit.*, p. 11.

30 *Ibid.*, pp. 69-70.

31 *The Sherborne Mercury*, January 1786.

32 Meriton, Henry and John Rogers, $$ cit, p. 11.

33 *Ibid.*, p. 11.

34 *Ibid.*, pp. 4-5.

35 *Ibid.*, pp. 70-1.

Chapter 8

1 Meriton, Henry, *A True and Particular Account of the Loss of the Halsewell*, p. 3

2 Thornton, Thomas (Editor), *Oriental Commerce, or the East India Trader's Complete Guide*, p. 130.

3 David J. Allen Archive, p. 68.

4 Wakeford, Joan, *Kingston's Past Rediscovered*, p. 78.

5 Meriton, Henry and John Rogers, *A Circumstantial Narrative of the Loss of the Halsewell*, p. 68.

6 Lipson, Ephraim, *Economic History of England*, p. 291.

7 Larn, Richard and Bridget, *Shipwreck Index of the British Isles*, Volume I, Section 6.

8 Oxford Dictionaries Online.

9 *London Recorder & Sunday Gazette*, 15 January 1786.

10 Chatterton, E. Keble, *A World for the Taking: The Ships of the Honourable East India Company*, pp. 152-3.

11 Meriton, Henry and John Rogers, *op. cit.*, p. 67. The inscription on Richard Peirce (junior's) tombstone—located in Calcutta's South Park Street Burial Ground—confirms that he was born in 1768.

12 Meriton, Henry, *op. cit.*, pp. 4-5.

13 Wakeford, Joan, *op. cit.*, (Information kindly supplied by the archivist, Tiffin School.)

14 Hardy, Charles and Horatio Charles Hardy, *A Register of Ships, Employed in the Service of the Honorable the United East India Company, from the year 1760 to 1810.*

15 Chatterton, E. Keble, *op. cit.*, p. 117.

16 Sutton, Jean, *Lords of the East: The East India Company and its Ships*, p. 104.

Chapter 9

1 Miller, Russell, *The East Indiamen*, p. 130.

2 Meriton, Henry and John Rogers, *A Circumstantial Narrative of the Loss of the Halsewell*, p. 9. Prior to *Halsewell*, the East Indiamen *General Goddard* and

HCS *Kent* had sailed through The Downs on 17 December 1785; *Sulivan* on 23 December, and *Manship* on 30 December. The next sailings after *Halsewell* were those of *Fort William* and *Valentine* (both to Coast & China), and *Phoenix* (to Coast & Bay), all on 16 January 1786, from Hardy, Charles and Horatio Charles Hardy, *A Register of Ships employed in the Service of the Honorable United East India Company from the year 1760-1810.*

3 *Ibid.*, p. 9.

4 *Ibid.*, p. 14.

5 The wooden sailing ship was prone to take in water at the best of times, either from sea spray or rain trickling down from above, or through gaps between the planks of her hull. In order to assess the depth of water in the bilges, a sounding tool—a long iron rod with notches at intervals of 1 inch, and attached to a small line, was used. The ship's carpenter would apply chalk to the rod, and then drop it down through a sounding pipe into the well. Hasluck, Paul N., *Cassell's Cyclopaedia of Mechanics.*

6 Meriton, Henry and John Rogers, *op. cit.*, pp. 14-15. Even in normal circumstances, the bilge well was sounded regularly, as a matter of course.

7 *Ibid.*, p. 16. Sited amidships, and above the lowest part of the hull, the so-called 'chain pump' consisted of a continuous chain which passed through a vertical pipe, downwards from the deck and into the bilge, and then back up to the deck through another pipe. At intervals along the length of the chain were 'valves', each consisting of several leather discs and metal backplate, attached to the chain above by a stirrup-shaped metal fitting. The chain was hauled upwards from the flooded bilge by means of a winch, complete with a long handle, in order that the strength of several men could be employed to operate it. In the process, water would be drawn into the pipe by suction and contained therein by the valves, as it made its way upwards to the deck, from where it would be left to drain away over the side through 'scuppers' (a scupper being a aperture in a ship's side designed to carry water overboard from the deck). Oertling, Thomas James, 'The History and Development of Ships' Bilge Pumps 1500-1840', A Thesis submitted to the Graduate College of Texas A&M University, pp. 73-97.

8 *Ibid.*, pp. 14-15.

9 *Ibid.*, pp. 16-18.

10 Information kindly supplied by Mark Rodaway OBE, of Her Majesty's Coastguard, Portland, Dorset.

11 It was

… early in the eighteenth century that Captain William Holman, supported by the shipowners and Corporation of Weymouth, put a petition to Trinity House [an association founded in 1514 which was responsible for the licensing of ships' pilots and for the construction and maintenance of buoys and lighthouses around the coasts of England and Wales] for the building of a lighthouse at Portland Bill. Trinity House opposed it, suggesting that lights at this point were needless and ship owners could not bear [afford] the burden of their upkeep. The people of Weymouth continued their petition and on 26th May, 1716,

Trinity House obtained a patent from George I. They in turn issued a lease for 61 years to a private consortium who built two lighthouses with enclosed lanterns and coal fires. The lights were badly kept, sometimes not lit at all. Transport Trust Heritage Site: Portland Bill Lighthouse (online).

It should be mentioned that at this point in history, the coastguard service had not evolved.

12 Meriton, Henry and John Rogers, *op. cit.*, p. 19.

13 *Ibid.*, pp. 18-19. Information kindly supplied by the United Kingdom Hydrographic Service.

14 Treves, Sir Frederick, *Highways and Byways of Dorset*, pp. 197-8. The 12th-century chapel described by Treves stands 441 feet above sea level. 32 feet square (externally), with walls 3½ feet thick, it is squat, and heavily buttressed with single doorway and Norman arch, single lancet window, and roof topped with a cross.

15 Meriton, Henry and John Rogers, *op. cit.*, p. 20.

16 Meriton, Henry, *A Circumstantial Narrative of the Loss of the Halsewell*, pp. 21-2.

Chapter 10

1 Treves, Sir Frederick, *Highways and Byways of Dorset*, p. 195.

2 Meriton, Henry and John Rogers, *A Circumstantial Narrative of the Loss of the Halsewell*, pp. 26-7.

3 *London Recorder & Sunday Gazette*, 15 January 1786.

4 Cunningham, George Godfrey (Editor), *Lives of Eminent and Illustrious Englishmen*, Volume VI, Part II, p. 439.

5 Fawcett, Sir Charles (Editor), *East Indiamen: The East India Company's Maritime Service*, p. 82.

6 Meriton, Henry and John Rogers, *op. cit.*, pp. 22-3.

7 *Ibid.*, pp. 23-4.

8 *Ibid.*, p. 27.

9 Chatterton, E. Keble, *A World for the Taking: The Ships of the Honourable East India Company*, p. 150.

10 Shipp, W., and J. W. Hodson (Editors), *The History and Antiquities of the County of Dorset* by John Hutchins, Volume I, p. 704.

11 Meriton, Henry and John Rogers, *op. cit.*, pp. 42-3.

Chapter 11

1 Meriton, Henry and John Rogers, *A Circumstantial Narrative of the Loss of the Halsewell*, pp. 41-4.

2 *Ibid.*, p. 44

3 *Ibid.*, p. 45. Meriton gives the first name of Mr Garland as George, which appears to be a mistake.

4 Treves, Sir Frederick, *Highways and Byways of Dorset*, p. 196.

5 Mee, Arthur, *The King's England: Dorset*, p. 320.

6 *Gentleman's Magazine*, Volume 59, London, John Nichols, 1786.

7 Meriton, Henry and John Rogers, *op. cit.*, pp. 46-7.

8 *Ibid.*, pp. 27-28.

9 In fact, the list of soldiers present appears on the HEIC's muster list, obtainable from the British Library. Whereas the HEIC's muster list states that 19 soldiers were saved, with the possibility that an additional 2 might have been saved, Meriton's list, indicates that 25 soldiers were saved.

10 Meriton, Henry, *A True and Particular Account of the Loss of the Halsewell*, pp. 54-5.

11 Meriton, Henry and John Rogers, *A Circumstantial Narrative of the Loss of the Halsewell*, pp. 45-6.

12 *Ibid.*, p. 50.

13 Hawker died on 2 September 1789 at Wareham, aged 51. Shipp, W., and J. W. Hodson (Editors), *The History and Antiquities of the County of Dorset* by John Hutchins, Volume 1, p. 112. N.B. No significance should be attached to the fact that Meriton referred to Hawker as 'Mr', because he referred to the Reverend Morgan Jones in the same way.

14 Meriton, Henry and John Rogers, *op. cit.*, p. 52.

15 The Reverend Morgan Jones, in Worth Matravers' Parish Register, 1786.

16 *The Times*, 10 January 1786.

Chapter 12

1 Meriton, Henry and John Rogers, *A Circumstantial Narrative of the Loss of the Halsewell*, pp. 62-3.

2 Extract of letter from the Revd Mr Geo. Ryves Hawker, Rector of Wareham, to Tho. Southcomb Esq. of Gate Street Lincolns Inn Fields, dated 9th Jan.y 1786. David J. Allen, Archive.

3 Meriton, Henry and John Rogers, *op. cit.*, pp. 63-4.

4 *Ibid.*, p. 63.

5 Of this tea set, only a single cup survives which, in 1974, was presented to Langton Matravers Parish Museum by Lieutenant Colonel Garland Jayne of Lisbon.

6 Information kindly supplied by Treleven Haysom.

7 *The Times*, 10 January 1786.

8 Cutwater—forward edge of the prow.

9 Letter from Mr T. M. Hardy from E. G. Hardy, dated 'Xmas 1939'. Information kindly supplied by David Haysom.

10 Published in the *Gentleman's Magazine*, 1786, Volume 59.

11 Carson, Edward, *The Ancient & Rightful Customs—a History of the English Customs Service*, p. 116.

12 *Hampshire Chronicle*, 18 December 1786, published in the *Gentleman's Magazine*, 1786, Volume 59.

13 Shipp, W., and J. W. Hodson (Editors), *The History and Antiquities of the County of Dorset* by John Hutchins, 3rd Edition, Volume I, p. 704.

14 Meriton, Henry and John Rogers, *op. cit.*, p. 54.

15 Purbeck Society Papers, 1856.

16 *The Times*, 10 January 1786.

17 'Narrative of the loss of the *Halsewell* Indiaman', *The Scots Magazine*, Volume 48, p. 22, January 1786, Edinburgh, Murray and Cochrane.

18 *Hampshire Chronicle*, 21 January 1786. Almost a century later, it was stated in the January–June 1863 edition of *Notes & Queries* that Captain Peirce's 'remains were never found'. *Notes & Queries* January–June 1863, London: Bell & Daldy.

19 Information kindly supplied by the Somerset and Dorset Family History Society. The 'West Cliff' probably relates to the cliffs at what later became the town of Bournemouth.

20 Christchurch Burial Records, Dorset Family History Centre.

21 Worth Matravers, Burials 1584-1841, transcript made by Mr Barry Chinchen from the original documents held at Dorset Record Office.

22 Christchurch Burial Records, Dorset Family History Centre.

23 *Hampshire Chronicle*, 13 February 1786

24 'Some Chronicles of the Larkins Family II: The Wreck of the *Halsewell*, 1786', by E. W. Bovill, FSA The Captain Thomas referred to was probably James, who is known to have served subsequently on HCS *Ponsborne*.

25 Meriton, Henry and John Rogers, *op. cit.*, p. 47.

26 *Ibid.*, p. 75-6.

27 *Ibid.*, pp. 73-4.

28 *Ibid.*, p. 51.

29 Public Record Office, Prob 11/1139.

Chapter 13

1 Information about tidal rates kindly supplied by the United Kingdom Hydrographic Office.

2 *Ibid.* N.B. The variation in the strength of tidal flow is predominantly dependent on the proximity of the Moon to the Earth, for when the moon's elliptical orbit takes it nearest to the Earth, this is when its gravitational pull on the sea is at its strongest. This produces the so-called 'spring tides', which occur just after a new or a full moon. Conversely 'neap tides' occur just after the first or third quarters of the moon, when the tidal flow is more moderate.

3 Oxford Dictionaries Online.

4 *Gentleman's Magazine*, January 1786, p. 44.

5 Information kindly supplied by the Meteorological Office Library & Archives.

6 Ledger of the *Ganges*, British Library, IOR/L/MAR/B/86S(1).

7 *Ganges, Journal*, July 27 1781 to 9 May 1785, British Library: IOR/L/MAR/B/86B.

8 Urban, Sylvanus, *Gentleman's Magazine*, Volume LVI, 1786, Part I, p. 174.

Chapter 14

1 *Gentleman's Magazine and Historical Chronicle*, 1856, Volume 56, Part 1.

2 Humphries, Mick, *The Halswell Family*, p. 12.

3 Silby, Jo (Editor), *The Goathurst Millennium Book: 1000 Years of Parish History*, pp. 63-6.

4 In 1671, Halswell Tynte (1649-1702) married Grace Fortecue, who bore him 6 children. On the death of his grandfather the Reverend Hugh Halswell in 1672, Halswell inherited Halswell Manor. On 7 June 1673, Halswell was created Baronet (member of the lowest hereditary titled British order.) Following in his father's footsteps in the elections of 1679, 1681 and 1685, he was elected MP for Bridgwater. On the death of Sir Halswell Tynte, 1st Baronet, in 1702, the estate and title were inherited by his eldest son John (1683-1710). Two years later, in 1704, Sir John Tynte (2nd Baronet), married Jane Kemeys, daughter and heiress of Charles Kemeys of Cefan Mably, Glamorganshire and his wife Mary, née Wharton. Jane bore him 3 sons and a daughter, Jane junior (1708-1741). On his death in 1710, Sir John was succeeded, in turn, by his eldest son Halswell (1705-1730, 3rd Baronet) and John (1707-1740, 4th Baronet and Rector of Goathurst). Halswell married Mary Walters, who bore him 2 daughters, both of whom died young. John did not marry, so on his death, the estate and title passed to his younger brother Charles, who adopted the surname 'Kemys Tynte'.

5 Burke, Sir Bernard, *A Genealogical and Heraldic History of the Landed Gentry of Great Britain and Northern Ireland*, Volume II, p. 1556.

6 Silby, Jo (Editor), *op. cit.*, pp. 63-6.

7 Pevsner, Nikolaus, *The Buildings of England: South and West Somerset*, pp. 188-9.

8 Silby, Jo (Editor), *op. cit.*, pp. 3-4.

9 Oxford Dictionaries Online.

10 Information kindly provided by Ann Manners.

Chapter 15

1 Hinchcliffe, John and Vicki, *Dive Dorset: A Diver Guide*, p. 157.

2 Information kindly supplied by Bob Errington.

3 In 1939, one and a half centuries later, it was reported that this bonnet was 'still in the possession of the family of the late Mr. Geo. Bishop, and several generations

of the family have been christened wearing it'. Letter from Mr T. M. Hardy from E. G. Hardy, dated 'Xmas 1939'. Information kindly supplied by David Haysom.

4 The mourning ring is believed to be in the possession of Colin Hobbs.

5 Information kindly supplied by Eric Youle.

6 'Britain's Sunken History', BBC 4, 9 December 2013.

7 Information kindly supplied by Wally Hammond.

8 Oxford Dictionaries Online

9 *Ibid.*

10 Information kindly supplied by Treleven Haysom.

11 Information kindly supplied by Royal Armories, Leeds, Yorkshire. Mystery musket: overall length 50½ inches; length of barrel 35½ inches; bore ¾ inch.

12 It has not been possible to discover more about this company.

13 Information kindly supplied by Bob Errington.

14 On 2 March 1784, French inventor and aviator Jean-Pierre Blanchard (1753-1809), made a successful balloon flight in Paris in a balloon filled with hydrogen gas and launched from the Champ de Mars. These early exploits triggered an outbreak of 'balloonomania', with exotically dressed balloonists setting forth in elaborately decorated and highly-coloured balloons. That August of 1784, Blanchard relocated to London, and on 7 January 1785, he and Dr John Jeffries of the USA, were the first to fly across the English Channel, from England to France—a voyage of about two-and-a-half hours duration.

15 McGilvary, George, *Guardian of the East India Company: the Life of Laurence Sulivan*, p. 67.

16 Marx, Karl, *The East India Company: Its History and Results, New York Herald Tribune*, 11 July 1853.

Chapter 16

1 Oxford Dictionaries Online.

2 *Ibid.*

3 Stephen, Sir Leslie, and Sir Sidney Lee, *The Dictionary of National Biography*, Oxford University Press, 1917.

4 The text for this version of 'Lewesdon Hill' is from the 1827 edition.

5 Darwin, Erasmus, *The Botanic Garden*, part I, canto iv.

Chapter 17

1 Meriton, Henry and John Rogers, *A Circumstantial Narrative of the Loss of the Halsewell*, pp. 1-2.

2 Oxford Dictionaries Online.

3 *The Times*, 6 March 1786.

4 'Going to the Movies in the Eighteenth Century: A Spectacle', by Collaboration at the ANU, posted online by Iain McCalman, Australian National University.

5 Shipp, W., and J. W. Hodson (Editors), *The History and Antiquities of the County of Dorset* by John Hutchins, volume 1, p. xx.

6 Hibbert, Christopher, *George III: A Personal History*, pp. 306-7.

7 Published in the *Western County Magazine*, October 1789.

8 The Royal family paid several subsequent visits to Weymouth. For example, in late June 1801, after a period of illness during which the King became delirious and aggressive, 'it was decided that he should convalesce at Weymouth, in the company of the Queen, the Princesses, and Prince Adolphus, then aged twenty-seven'. Hibbert, Christopher, *George III: A Personal History*, pp. 318-9.

9 Kollmann, A. F. C., published by Corri, Dussek, & Co. of London, in ? 1796. Information kindly supplied by the University of Cambridge, where a copy of the work currently resides: Item No. 11 in Volume MR340.a.75.46.

10 Dickens, Charles (Editor), *All The Year Round*, pp. 347-52.

11 Dickens, Charles, 'The Long Voyage', *Household Words*, 31 December 1853.

Chapter 18

1 National Maritime Museum.

2 Oxford Dictionaries Online.

3 Having trained at the Royal Academy, J. M. W. Turner concentrated on landscapes and seascapes. He

... had a restless temperament [and] travelled constantly... above all, he was excited by nature: the thrill of overwhelming natural forces, delight in nature's delicate sweetness, and the crowning magnificence of sunlight.

In his exploration of the possibilities of using colour to express mood, Turner was fortunate in that, during his lifetime, 'scientific and technical advances produced new pigments and dyes' which he was able to make use of'. (Cumming, Robert, *Annotated Great Artists*, pp. 66-7.) In 1796 his first oil painting entitled 'Fishermen at Sea', was exhibited at the Royal Academy.
Turner travelled widely throughout Britain and also on the Continent. In 1811 he was commissioned by engraver and publisher W.B. Cooke, to produce forty drawings for a work which would be entitled *Views of the Southern Coast of England*. To this end, during that July and August, he duly familiarized himself with the coast of Dorsetshire, Devonshire, Cornwall and Somersetshire, in the course of which he made more than 200 pencil sketches. (Lindsay, Jack, *Turner: The Man and his Art*, p. 70.)
In his later works, Turner favoured 'impressions' rather than detail, as, for example, when he portrays the effect of light on water. (In this respect, he was to influence the French impressionists and in particular Claude Monet, who studied his technique.)

His imagination was fuelled by natural catastrophes, and shipwrecks in particular. For example, 'Dawn after the Wreck' and 'The Slave Ship', both painted in 1840, reflect his fascination with the violent power of the sea.

4 Shanes, Eric, *Turner's Watercolour Explorations 1810–1842*, pp. 33-5.
5 Thornbury, Walter, *The Life of J. M. W. Turner*, p. 205.
6 *Ibid.*, p. 209.

Chapter 19

1 Oxford Dictionaries Online.
2 Volume II of *A Topographical History of Surrey* by E. W. Brayley contains an engraving from 1840 of the interior of All Saints Church, Kingston-upon-Thames, in which no less than seven hatchments are depicted. Of these all but one were subsequently removed, including that relating to Captain Peirce. Information kindly supplied by the Reverend Jonathan Wilkes.
3 From 'Bengal Obituary', a compilation made in 1848, information kindly supplied by Richard Daglish.
4 *Notes & Queries*, January–June 1863, London, Bell & Daldy.
5 Wakeford, Joan, *Kingston's Past Rediscovered*, pp. 78-80.
6 Information kindly supplied by John King, archivist, Tiffin School.
7 Hardy, Charles and Horatio Charles Hardy, *A Register of Ships, Employed in the Service of the Honorable the United East India Company, from the year 1760 to 1810.*
8 Josselyn, the Reverend Edward, *Memorials to Serve for a History of the Parish of Rotherhythe*, based on Joseph Allen, *Battles of the British Navy*, Volume II, pp. 12-13.
9 Oxford Dictionaries Online.
10 Miller, Russell, *The East Indiamen*, p. 155.
11 Josselyn, the Reverend Edward, *op. cit.*, Volume II, pp. 78-80.
12 Information kindly supplied by Thomas Del Mar of London.
13 Cotton, Sir Evan, *East Indiamen*, p. 174.
14 Farrington, Anthony, *A Biographical Index of East India Company Maritime Service Officers 1600–1834.*
15 John Daniel's name does not appear in the above *Biographical Index* after 1786.
16 Old Bailey proceedings (online), 25 October 1786. Reference no: t17861025-34.
17 Oxford Dictionaries Online.
18 *The Times*, 6 December 1843.
19 *Notes & Queries*, January–June 1863. London: Bell & Daldy, 1863. Entry dated 10 January 1863, p. 34.
20 The ring was included in a bequest of micro-carved ivories collected by D. M. W. Bullock and left to the museum in 1918. Information kindly supplied by Bristol Museum & Art Gallery.
21 Richard Daglish to the author, 27 September 2016.
22 David J. Allen Archive.
23 Lenman, Bruce P. (Consultant Editor), *Chambers Dictionary of World History.*

Epilogue

1 Crowe, William, 'Lewesdon Hill'.

Appendix 1

1 Larn, Richard and Bridget, *Shipwreck Index of the British Isles*, Volume I, Section 6.
2 Matthew, H. C. G., and Brian Harrison (Editors) *Oxford Dictionary of National Biography*.
3 *Ibid*.

Appendix 2

1 Hardy, Charles and Horatio Charles Hardy, *A Register of Ships, Employed in the Service of the Honorable the United East India Company, from the year 1760 to 1810*, p. 111.

Appendix 3

1 Hardy, Charles and Horatio Charles Hardy, *A Register of Ships, Employed in the Service of the Honorable the United East India Company, from the year 1760 to 1810*, p. 179.

N.B. The Rules and Regulations of the East India Company, in respect of ships, captains, crews, and trade, amounted to over 60 pages. Although this extract is from the Register of 1804, it is likely that the same conditions applied during the latter part of the eighteenth century, at the time of Captain Peirce and HCS *Halsewell*.

Appendix 4

1 Hardy, Charles and Horatio Charles Hardy, *A Register of Ships, Employed in the Service of the Honorable the United East India Company, from the year 1760 to 1810, with an Appendix, containing a Variety of Particulars, and Useful Information interesting to those concerned with East India Commerce*, pp. 74-5.

The definition of various terms found in literature pertaining to the East India Company, have virtually all been obtained from *Oxford Dictionaries* online.

Appendix 5

1 Information kindly supplied by Victoria & Albert Museum.
2 John Hamilton Moore (*c.* 1738-1807) of Tower-Hill, London, was born Edinburgh. A teacher of Navigation, his *Epitome* was first published in 1772 as *The Practical Navigator and New Daily Assistant.* Later editions were renamed *The New Practical Navigator, being an Epitome of Navigation.*
3 *The Midshipman's or British Mariner's Vocabulary; being a Universal Dictionary of Technical Terms and Sea Phrases used in the Construction, Equipment, Management and Military Operations of a Ship,* by J. J. Moore, first published in 1769.
4 Hardy, Charles and Horatio Charles Hardy, A Register of Ships, Employed in the Service of the Honorable the United East India Company, from the year 1760 to 1810, pp. 148-9.

Appendix 6

1 Hardy, Charles and Horatio Charles Hardy, A Register of *Ships, Employed in the Service of the Honorable the United East India Company, from the year 1760 to 1810,* pp. 66-9.

Appendix 7

1 Hardy, Charles and Horatio Charles Hardy, A Register of Ships, Employed in the Service of the Honorable the United East India Company, from the year 1760 to 1810, pp. 74-5.

Appendix 8

1 Meriton, Henry and John Rogers, *A Circumstantial Narrative of the Loss of the Halsewell,* pp. 56-7.

Appendix 9

1 Reference BL-OIOC, Ref L/MIL//9/91.

Appendix 10

1 Hardy, Charles and Horatio Charles Hardy, *A Register of Ships, Employed in the Service of the Honorable the United East India Company, from the year 1760 to 1810,* p. 80.

2 British Library, *Halsewell Journal*, L/MAR/B/465A-B.

3 Hardy, Charles and Horatio Charles Hardy, *op. cit.*, p. 98.

4 British Library, *Halsewell Journal*, L/MAR/B/465C.

5 Hardy, Charles and Horatio Charles Hardy, *op. cit.*, p. 111.

Appendix 12

1 Hardy, Charles and Horatio Charles Hardy, *A Register of Ships, Employed in the Service of the Honorable the United East India Company, from the year 1760 to 1810*, pp. 73-4.

Appendix 13

1 Meriton, Henry and John Rogers, *A Circumstantial Narrative of the Loss of the Halsewell*, pp. 58-62.

Appendix 14

1 Wakeford, Joan, *Kingston's Past Rediscovered*, p. 78 and information kindly supplied by John King, archivist, Tiffin School.

Bibliography

ALLEN, Joseph, *Battles of the British Navy* (Henry G. Bohm, London, 1852)

BIRDWOOD, Sir George Christopher Molesworth, *Report on the Old Records of the India Office*, W. H. Allen, London, and at Calcutta, 1891.

BOWMAN, Florence L., and Esther G. Roper, *Traders in East and West* (The Sheldon Press, London, 1924)

BROUGH, Anthony, *Considerations on the Necessity of Lowering the Exorbitant Freight of Ships employed in the Service of the East-India Company* (C.G.J. and J. Robinson, London, 1786)

BURKE, Sir Bernard, *A Genealogical and Heraldic History of the Landed Gentry of Great Britain and Northern Ireland*, Harrison, London, 1863.

CHATTERTON, E. Keble, *A World for the Taking: The Ships of the Honourable East India Company* (Fireship Press, Tucson, Arizona, USA, 2008)

CHATTERTON, E. Keble, *The Old East Indiamen* (Conway Maritime, London, 1971)

COOKE, W. B. and George Cooke, *Picturesque Views on the Southern Coast of England* (John & Arthur Arch, London, 1814)

COTTON, Sir Evan, *East Indiamen* (The Blatchworth Press, London, 1949)

CUMMING, Robert, *Annotated Great Artists* (Dorling Kindersley, London, 2000)

CUNNINGHAM, George Godfrey (Editor), *Lives of Eminent and Illustrious Englishmen*, Volume VI, Part II (Fullarton, Glasgow, 1826)

DARWIN, Erasmus, *The Botanic Garden* (J. Johnson, London, 1791)

DAVIS, Terence, *Wareham: Gateway to Purbeck* (Dorset Publishing Company, Wincanton, Somerset, 1984)

DICKENS, Charles (Editor), *All The Year Round* (Chapman & Hall, London, 1866-1867)

FARRINGTON, Anthony, *A Biographical Index of East India Company Maritime Service Officers 1600-1834*, (The British Library, London, 1999)

FAWCETT, Sir Charles (Editor), *East Indiamen: The East India Company's Maritime Service*, by Sir Evan Cotton (Blatchworth, London, 1949)

GARDINER, Samuel Rawson, *A School Atlas of English History* (Longmans, Green, London, 1907)

HARDY, Charles and HARDY, Horatio Charles, *A Register of Ships, Employed in the Service of the Honorable the United East India Company, from the year 1760 to 1810: with an Appendix, containing a Variety of Particulars, and Useful Information interesting to those concerned with East India Commerce* (Black, Parry, and Kingsbury, London, 1811)

HASLUCK, Paul N., *Cassell's Cyclopaedia of Mechanics* (Cassell, London, 1908)

HIBBERT, Christopher, *George III: A Personal History* (Viking, London, 1998)

HINCHCLIFFE, John and Vicki, *Dive Dorset: A Diver Guide* (Underwater World Publications, Teddington, Middlesex, UK, 1999)

HUMPHRIES, Mick, *The Halswell Family* (May 2014 edition).

JOSSELYN, Reverend Edward, *Memorials to Serve for a History of the Parish of Rotherhythe* (Cambridge University Press, 1907)

KOLLMANN, A. F. C., *Opera VI* (Corri, Dussek, & Co., London, ?1796)

LARN, Richard and Bridget *Shipwreck Index of the British Isles*, Volume I (Lloyds Registry of Shipping, London, 1994)

LEGG, Rodney, *Corfe Castle Encyclopaedia* (Dorset Publishing Company, Wincanton, Somerset, 2000)

LEGG, Rodney, *Guide to Purbeck Coast and Shipwreck* (Dorset Publishing Company, Sherborne, Dorset, 1984)

LENMAN, Bruce P. (Consultant Editor), *Chambers Dictionary of World History* (Chambers Harrap Publishers, Edinburgh and New York, 2000)

LINDSAY, Jack, *Turner: The Man and his Art* (Granada, London, 1985)

LIPSON, Ephraim, *Economic History of England* (A. & C. Black, London, 1931)

MARX, Karl, *The East India Company: Its History and Results*, New York Herald Tribune.

MATTHEW, H. C. G., and Brian Harrison (Editors), *Oxford Dictionary of National Biography* (Oxford University Press, 2004)

McGILVARY, George, *Guardian of the East India Company: the Life of Laurence Sulivan* (Taurus Academic Studies, London, 2006)

MEE, Arthur, *The King's England: Dorset* (Hodder and Stoughton, London, 1959)

MERITON, Henry and ROGERS, John, *A Circumstantial Narrative of the Loss of the Halsewell* (William Lane, London, 1786)

MERITON, Henry (the presumed author), *Remarkable Shipwrecks: or A Collection of Interesting Accounts of Naval Disasters* (Andrus and Starr, Hartford, Connecticut, USA, 1813). (The relevant chapter in this volume is a précis of *A Circumstantial Narrative of the Loss of the Halsewell*, by Meriton)

MERITON, Henry, *A True and Particular Account of the Loss of the Halsewell* (R. Raworth, London, 1786). (This account is very similar to *A Circumstantial Narrative of the Loss of the Halsewell*, by Meriton and Rogers, with a few additions. Meriton is therefore the presumed author, possibly with contributions from others.

MILLER, David, *The World of Jack Aubrey* (Salamander, London, 2003)

MILLER, Russell, *The East Indiamen* (Time/Life Books, Amsterdam, 1980)

'Monody on the Death of Captain Peirce, and those Unfortunate Young Ladies who Perished with Him, in the *Halsewell* East Indiaman', memorial poem (1790) by an unknown author (W. Lane, London, 1790)

NICHOLAS, Thomas, *Annals and Antiquities of the Counties and County Families of Wales* (Longmans, Green, Reader, 1872)

O'KEEFFE, John, *Recollections of the Life of John O'Keeffe* (Henry Colburn, London, 1826)

PARTRIDGE, Eric, *A Dictionary of Slang and Unconventional English* (Routledge, London, 2000)

PEIRCE, Captain Richard, *Journal 1778-82*, British Library, L/MAR/B/465A-B

PEIRCE, Captain Richard, *Journal 1782-84*, British Library, L/MAR/B/465C

PEVSNER, Nikolaus, *The Buildings of England: South and West Somerset* (Penguin, 1958)

POCOCK, Tom, *Horatio Nelson* (Bockhampton Press, London, 1999)

RAINE, Matthew, 'A Sermon, preached at Kingston-upon-Thames, on Sunday February 19, 1786, upon the Death of Captain Richard Peirce', by the Rev. Matthew Raine, A. M. ('Artium Magister'—Master of Arts), Fellow of Trinity College, Cambridge (G. Kearsley, London, 1786)

RAWLINSON, H. G., *British Beginnings in Western India, 1579-1657: An Account of the Early Days of the British Factory of Surat* (Clarendon Press, Oxford, 1920)

RAWLINSON, H. G., *India: A Short Cultural History* (The Cresset Press, London, 1952)

SCOT, Elizabeth, *Alonzo and Cora* (Bunney & Gold, London, 1801)

SHANES, Eric, *Turner's Watercolour Explorations 1810-1842* (Tate Gallery Publishing, London, 1997)

SHIPP, W. and HODSON, J. W., (Editors), *The History and Antiquities of the County of Dorset*, by John Hutchins, 3rd Edition, Wakefield, Yorkshire (EP Publishing Ltd, in collaboration with Dorset County Library, 1868)

SILBY, Jo (Editor). *The Goathurst Millennium Book: 1000 Years of Parish History* (The Goathurst Millennium Book Publication Group, 2000)

SPENCER, Alfred (Editor), *Memoirs of William Hickey* (Hurst & Blackett, London, 1913-1925)

STEPHEN, Sir Leslie, and LEE, Sir Sidney, *The Dictionary of National Biography* (Oxford University Press, 1917)

SUTTON, Jean, *Lords of the East: The East India Company and its Ships* (Conway Maritime Press, London, 1981)

THOMAS, Evan, 'The Shipwreck of the *Halsewell* East-Indiaman: a Poem, With Very Copious and Authentic Notes, Giving a Full Account of that Very Melancholy Catastrophe, From the Sailing of the Vessel, Jan. 1st, to its Destruction, Jan. 6th, 1786, to which is added, a Consolatory Address' (printed by T. Wood, Shrewsbury, Shropshire, ?1786)

THORNBURY, Walter, *The Life of J. M. W. Turner* (Chatto & Windus, London, 1897)

THORNTON, Thomas (Editor), *Oriental Commerce, or the East India Trader's Complete Guide*, by

William Milburn (Kingsbury, Parbury & Allen, London, 1825)

TREVES, Sir Frederick, *Highways and Byways of Dorset* (Macmillan, London, 1906)

URBAN, Sylvanus (Editor), *Gentleman's Magazine* (David Henry, London, 1786)

WAKEFORD, Joan, *Kingston's Past Rediscovered* (Phillimore, Stroud, Gloucestershire, 1990)

WATSON, J. Steven, *The Reign of George III* (Clarendon Press, Oxford, 1960)

Index